PRAISE FOR T...
DRESS RE...

'An essential guide for all ambitious young people searching to reach their dreams and give them confidence to lead their life as upstanders not bystanders.'
– Paul Stewart, former racing driver, Formula 1 Team co-founder: Stewart Grand Prix

'*This Is Not a Dress Rehearsal* shines a motivational light on the link between happiness and success. Written with charming humility by a man preeminent in his field, it balances personal anecdotes with philosophical musings to serve up an espresso to dozing ambition.'
– Jonathan Kilmartin, former Senior Vice President Strategy and Consultancy, IMG

'In a world full of challenges, Michel's story is quite unique. He provides genuine illustrations and advice on how to push yourself to become an achiever. Michel and I share the view that anyone can create a positive impact should they invest enough of their passion and determination.'

'Michel is an exception to the rules. In an industry where the fast lane and sharp elbows create prestige and influence as a rule, he has remained one thing above all – human. Michel's story is an inspiration and encouragement as well as an example of loyalty and humility. I put his book in the heart of my kids.'

'Michel's journey is a tale in and of itself. This book is worth reading simply for his anecdotes, be they personal or from the upper echelons of the sports and business worlds. Michel is a true flag-carrier of the spirit my dad communicated in his bestselling book, *What They Don't Teach You at Harvard Business School*. I am so pleased that through *This Is Not a Dress Rehearsal*, Michel perpetuates the McCormack family legacy to generations to come.'

– Leslie McCormack, former Senior International Vice President, IMG, Daughter of IMG founder, Mark McCormack

'A modern-day Tintin who inspires us to travel and see the world from a different perspective. An inspiration for us all!'

– Nick Rodwell, Head of Studio Hergé

'For any young person feeling uncertain about their future or challenged about the lack of opportunities, this book is like a shot of passionate adrenaline. I share Michel's motto to live life to the fullest and make the most of what you have starting from being positive and believing in yourself.'

– Tom Kristensen, racing driver, record 9 times winner of the 24 Hours of Le Mans, FIA World Endurance Champion and Hall of Fame

'What an entertaining inspiration... I enjoyed every chapter, every story and every message. Michel motivates us to go for it, search for purpose in our own lives. I met Michel professionally but am proud to call him my friend, and I look up to him as a father who was brave enough to leave his legacy behind!'

– Norbert Teufelburger, entrepreneur and investor, co-founder and former CEO of Bwin

'Our movement empowers children to rise above their challenges and find their way back to hope. Michel's story shares this same philosophy. His book is inspirational, it will give confidence to the next generation to create their own success story.'

– Susan McIsaac, President and CEO, Right to Play International, former Managing Director, Strategic Philanthropy at Royal Bank of Canada

'A journey of discovery, of understanding risk, of boldness in the face of doubt.

This is a book which makes one pause – time after time – and truly understand the principles upon which the world operates. Michel also explains why the institutions of learning fall short in giving tools for real success. The doers of this world count on belief, faith and optimism with an abundance of passion to do incredible, impossible things. Masquelier gives you the road map with great stories of how it worked for him – and it did work for him! I witnessed his leadership delivering:

1. extraordinary results, which engendered...
2. loyalty from large organizations which (prior to him) were lacking in any soul – and...
3. cultural enthusiasm, which meant that they...
4. suddenly dominated their competition and recruited the best talent in the space.

This is a rare look into the mind and heart of one GREAT leader. If you want to make a difference, or just rise to the top in your chosen field of true endeavor, this is the book for you. Don't miss it.'

– Dave Checketts, managing partner at Checketts Partners Investment Management, former CEO of Madison Square Garden, former President of New York Knicks

THIS IS NOT A DRESS REHEARSAL

A short course in writing your own script
for success in business and life

MICHEL MASQUELIER

First published in Great Britain by Practical Inspiration Publishing, 2022

© Michel Masquelier, 2022

The moral rights of the author have been asserted.

ISBN   9781788603119   (print)
       9781788603133   (epub)
       9781788603126   (mobi)

To Charlotte, Alice and Louis. I have written
This Is Not a Dress Rehearsal for you, my
three beloved children. The idea is to inspire,
stimulate, and help you shape your destiny. If
you wish to contribute to the meaningfulness of
my journey, and prolong my spiritual existence,
show me I have provided you with wisdom and
inspiration.

CONTENTS

ABOUT THE AUTHOR

Michel Masquelier is the former chairman of IMG Media, part of the largest sports management agency and a fortune 500 company.

Masquelier spent 35 years at the heart of the sports industry, working with organizations such as the Olympic games, Wimbledon and the Premier League. His work has brought him into contact with some of the most famous athletes in history, CEOs of blue-chip companies, as well as some of the pioneers of the media industry.

Having graduated with a degree in Law from a university in Belgium, he moved to London to work his way up the ladder at IMG from intern to chairman. He built a worldwide team that shook up the business of sport, with revolutionary commercial concepts and innovative business models.

One of the most charismatic, influential and respected figures in the industry, he now takes on the role of advisor to governing bodies, media organizations and private equity firms. Michel is still a compulsive networker, but his passion has shifted to stimulating education, especially amongst future generations.

In the same spirit of innovation and disruption, he is involved in philanthropic projects, motivational speaking and development of educational programs for young executives. He is married with three children and lives in Switzerland.

ACKNOWLEDGEMENTS

This book would not have been possible without help from many people. I would like to thank my daughters Charlotte and Alice for helping me get this project off the ground and their initial enthusiasm. I would like to place on record my gratitude to the late Kevin Roberts, who helped me shape the early chapters of the book. My thanks to Frank Dunne for providing patient editorial guidance and advice throughout this project. Thanks also to Becki Bush for her suggestions about how to improve the book and her eye for detail in editing the first draft. The support and encouragement of Alison Jones and her team, of Practical Inspiration Publishing, have been invaluable. Finally, special mention is due to all the incredible friends and colleagues I was privileged to know at IMG over a period of more than 30 years. Some of them are mentioned in the book, but there are many others to whom I will always be grateful. And last, but not least, a very special thanks to my wife Sarah, who makes everything possible.

Most of this book is drawn from memory. Any errors or oversights are my own.

The author's royalties from this book will go to Right to Play, a charitable organization that harnesses the power of play and sport to educate some of the world's most vulnerable children in some of the world's most challenging situations.

INTRODUCTION

This Is Not a Dress Rehearsal is a series of real-life experiences, philosophical reflections, observations and intuitions. I hope they will help you to achieve things beyond your expectations, to spur you on your journey and enable you to stand out from the crowd.

There is something I would like to stress from the outset. Everybody is unique and everybody's journey through life is different. I have been able to benefit from opportunities at various points in my life that others may never have had. I have benefited from good fortune on many occasions. Maybe I was born under a lucky star. And maybe I grew up at a time when some things were possible which no longer are. I would not presume to extrapolate from my own existence a template or a model, or some prescriptive set of rules, that will work for everyone or that will guarantee success in work or life. This is not a roadmap for how you should live your life. This is one person's story, and I believe I have been honest about myself in this book. If there is even one thing that you can take away from it that gives you hope or encouragement – or makes you feel less alone on your journey – then the effort will have been worthwhile.

But I *do* believe that wherever you start from and whatever your circumstances, you have a choice in life. Either you motivate yourself to control your future, to search for success and contentment, or you let your life be determined by the elements. If you choose the former, then these reflections are for you – for those who believe they can be the masters of their own destiny. This book is not for the bystanders. It is for those who want to make a difference and leave a legacy.

It is all intended to help you boost your confidence, stimulate your appetite for adventure and capitalize on your inner talents. There is nothing here I would not say to my own children.

You are an actor dropped live onto the stage. There is no script. There is no dress rehearsal. It is all happening in real time. Before you realize it, you can be confined to playing a role that does not fit you – a role dictated by your environment or by other people, a role that does not fulfil you. But you can transcend this to become who you know you can be.

People are social animals, and we instinctively want to protect ourselves. Broadly speaking, we do what we are told, and we are naturally fearful when confronted with the unknown. We're prone to following the crowd – because the crowd is usually the safest place – and are incentivized to be good citizens. Most of us are naturally risk-averse most of the time, and want to live in a safe, controlled environment. We follow the rules of our society – written and unwritten. There's nothing wrong with any of this – it's a natural instinct, and part of what makes us human – but it can mean that we end up cast in a role that's been scripted by someone else. However, we *do* have a choice.

I've been called lots of things: a rebel, an innovator, an adventurer, a non-conformist and more. Some of these are more flattering names than others, of course, but they all came about because I strongly desired to be the captain of my own life; I wanted to write my own script and decide who I was going to be and how. I am still absolutely determined to live my passion, and I will let nothing get in the way of that.

There's more than just determination, too: I am also convinced that our time on the stage should be fun. There is a form of contentment to be had that is not defined by professional or material success, and does not rely on painful sacrifices or making compromises.

Time is life's most valuable commodity. Don't waste it playing the wrong role.

CHAPTER 1

WHERE THERE'S A WILL, THERE'S A WAY: TAKING TO THE STAGE

Let's set the scene. It's summer 2013. As the sun sets over Manhattan, I'm looking out across Times Square from the global headquarters of Morgan Stanley. The bank is one of two financial institutions, along with Evercore Partners, that has been appointed to sell IMG Worldwide, the world's largest sports management agency.

There are maybe 20 people in the lavishly appointed boardroom. Representatives of the two banks and the heads of all IMG divisions are on one side of the room. On the other are executives from the talent representation agency William Morris Endeavor (WME) and their team of bankers, analysts, lawyers and consultants.

It's not hard to see why IMG is such a catch. The company represents and manages the world's greatest athletes and fashion icons, stages hundreds of live sports events globally every year, is the largest independent producer and distributor of sports media globally and represents the interests of the most famous sport federations. This is the latest meeting in the 'road show' organized by IMG's owners, private equity firm Forstmann Little & Company. For the last few weeks, between the offices of Morgan Stanley and Evercore, we have been making our pitch to a dozen or so of the biggest venture capital firms in the world.

My part is explaining the segment I manage: IMG Media, the very attractive, fastest-growing division of the organization. I am almost certainly the only person in the room who has grown up not speaking English. At first the presentations were a little daunting, but now I'm in my stride, enjoying the process. I'm on my feet, running through my slide deck, laying out my vision of where this business is heading. The Q&A that follows is forensic in its detail.

There's definitely an appetite in the financial world for a business that brings together the number one passion point for nearly everyone – sport – with media, the vehicle that brings it into our homes. There's also appetite for a business that delivers continuous growth. But I notice something different about the team from WME: their hunger seems keener, their passion more palpable. Everything about their approach shouts 'more!'

If you are familiar with Ari Emanuel, chief executive of WME, this hunger and passion is not surprising. You may not know the name, but you might well know Ari Gold, the uber-agent from LA-based comedy-drama series *Entourage*, whose larger-than-life character was based heavily on Emanuel. The real Ari is a visionary who has long harboured the desire to marry the world's largest sports management company with the world's largest talent representation company. To make that happen, he has brought in the financial backing of Silver Lake, a technology investment firm with over US$75 billion of assets under its management.

In the end, it takes just a few weeks for the lawyers to iron out the contract wrinkles before we can unveil one of the biggest mergers in entertainment history: WME and Silver Lake have paid US$2.4 billion to buy IMG.

It has been an incredible journey for me. Working at IMG has been a mind-blowing experience and I've been living my passion every day. But for a moment, while rubbing shoulders with these high-flying financiers, I can't help thinking back. My journey here, to one of the high points in my career, was not a straight line. In that moment, I marvel at all the twists and turns and think back to the first tentative steps I took on that journey, 30 years earlier.

Going is easy, leaving is harder

Only 84 miles (135 kilometres) of English Channel separate the Belgian port-town of Zeebrugge from Dover in England, but as I closed the door on my battered Ford Escort and climbed the stairs from the ferry's car deck towards the passenger lounges, the distance could have been a million miles and I wouldn't have cared. With my few belongings in the old banger, and just enough money to last a month, I knew this was a journey where the destination was not just England, but my future. Just four and a half hours at sea separated the life I had known and the life I wanted. The fact that I spoke not a word of English and had no friends to welcome me and nowhere to stay didn't matter. What counted was that I was on my way. I had no fear, no apprehension, just a big heart.

I am from Liège, Belgium, a small town in a small country. Until the day I set out for England, I'd lived a reasonably comfortable life. I certainly didn't feel it was my destiny to be thrown onto the world stage and embrace an international management career. I had struggled to pass my law degree, but it was a degree that would have guaranteed me a reasonable job and a steady career. My uncle was a successful notary in my hometown, where our family was known and respected. The road had been mapped out for me: *Tonton* Yves was going to take me under his wing, and ultimately I would succeed him. I would have been able to afford a comfortable lifestyle, with time to socialize with friends. I would have met a fiancée from a similar background and raised a nice family on my home soil.

For many, such an outcome might seem a great achievement on all fronts. But it was not my calling. It may have been the destiny others planned for me, but it was never one I was going to endorse. I could hear the call of a different kind of life and so I found the energy and courage to avoid the safe but ultimately unsatisfying future and embark on a more challenging path. I wanted to see the world, to fly the nest and live the life of an adventurer. I put the degree I had grafted for aside so I could live my passion. I was determined to give it a shot.

My favourite poet and singer-songwriter is that rarest of things: a Belgian role model. His name is Jacques Brel. He was a constant source of inspiration to me – a true rebel who thrived on challenges. Brel once said, 'What is difficult for a guy from Vilvoorde who wants to go to Hong Kong is not going to Hong Kong but leaving Vilvoorde.' Vilvoorde is a very small town in Flemish-speaking Belgium; even if you don't know it (and you probably don't!) you'll know somewhere like it. Every country has its Vilvoordes. Going *to* England was easy for me, in some ways, but leaving home was hard.

However, a determination to succeed had encouraged me to set my course for England and a new life. I was facing more uncertainty than I had ever encountered, but I summoned all my resolve: I would allow no barrier to prevent me from realizing my dream and breaking the mould which had shaped my life, whether that was my lack of English, my lack of money or the very real prospect of loneliness.

Widen your stage

Throughout my early years, I had suffered – as many people do – from the claustrophobic restrictions of society and the school system. Have you ever been told you are not good enough – not good enough at school, not good enough at work? Have you ever been told you are not good enough by a sports coach, or even by your parents? Perhaps you have been told this so much that you have begun to doubt yourself and your own abilities. I've certainly been there – especially as a teen.

But in my early twenties, I found my own sense of direction. Part of this discovery I attribute to a widening of my world – especially formative for me was a month-long visit to the United States during one summer at university. In our little world, the United States was a kind of Promised Land, a place I had to see. I arrived on the East Coast, then went where the wind blew me. Bourbon Street in New Orleans, the mecca of jazz. Then a Greyhound bus to California, where distant cousins of my family had a son playing professional tennis.

From there, another Greyhound to the south of the state, and a visit to friends of these cousins who had a ranch close to the Mexican border. It was meant to be just a hospitality stop, but I asked for a job and they gave me one. For two weeks, I would spend the whole day with the mostly Mexican workforce, digging out weeds from a vast bean plantation. I loved hanging out with them after work, swimming in rivers and driving in their incredible pimped-up rides, with their giant horns at the front. We'd walk for miles across the ranch picking those weeds, followed by our own mobile toilet. You can imagine how it looked by the end of the day, and as the young, visiting newbie, you know who drew the short straw! I was there with a hose, blasting away. It was one of those rites-of-passage moments that I would often think back on later in my career to remind myself how far I had come.

From the fields of south California, via the casinos of Las Vegas and Los Angeles, and then a flight to New York. Wow! This was a different world again: the noise, the sirens, the hustle and bustle. I was like a kid in a candy store! A month later, I returned home to finish my studies, but this trip had ignited my wanderlust, and proved to me that discovery was written in my DNA.

When the time came for me to make my big move, it could easily have been another trans-Atlantic journey, given the impression that the United States had made on me. But it wasn't. I was drawn to England because of its lifestyle and its culture. I loved the rock bands, the provocative fashions, the sport and that uniquely British mixture of the traditional and the avant-garde. As a youngster, I had been able to pick up a signal to the BBC. It was a window onto a world of the Rolling Stones, Benny Hill, Manchester United. I was astounded by the endless coverage of cricket on prime-time national television. And snooker – a sport I did not even know existed. Everything was iconic and inspirational to me. I was also captivated by the British sense of humour, something I shared with my friends, which was evident whenever we got together.

Departure had meant saying goodbye to my family. I still recall the profound disappointment on my father's face: he simply didn't understand what I was doing, or why. He was hoping I would live the life he had lived, and in bilingual Belgium, his priority for me was to learn Flemish rather than English. With his friends ready to take me on as a trainee in a major insurance company, he could not understand why I did not capitalize on my hard-earned degree to start a career straight away. He saw the world through the lens of his own experience and felt I was wasting years during which I could have been earning towards a big pension and my retirement package. Now I recognize the sense in that viewpoint – even if I don't necessarily agree with it still – but back then I was just starting my life. Thinking about the end of it was the last thing I wanted to do!

An inspiring legacy

My father was strict when it came to good manners, but he could be overpowering at times and he wasn't the greatest listener. He was risk-averse. Our perspectives of the world clashed. My mother, on the other hand, embraced my adventurous vison of the world. She had lived through a more challenging upbringing, having been raised in Africa.

There was one relative I took positive inspiration from: my maternal grandfather, Nicolas Guillaume. He was a true adventurer, a risk-taker and a positive thinker. 'Bon Papa' came from a modest farming family in Lanaye in Belgium, a tiny village on an island in the river Meuse, south of Maastricht. He was one of three sons. Only one of his brothers was sent to school, which was something of a privilege in that area. He and the other two had to make their own way and learn from the world around them.

Nicolas became an entrepreneur, learning the trade of road building in rural Wallonia, the French-speaking region in the south of Belgium. He lived through World War II and had to get into all sorts of chicanery and wheeling and dealing to survive the German occupation. He never said as much, but we were fairly sure he had been a partisan – a member of the resistance. That generation didn't talk about their war experiences much.

In 1949, *Bon Papa* took his family to what was known in those days as the Belgian Congo, and what today is called the Democratic Republic of the Congo. He had no job to go to, but from a hotel in Kinshasa, the capital city, he began making contacts and establishing himself. Gradually, he started winning contracts to build roads across the country. His major breakthrough was the deal to build a military base at Kamina, in the deep south of the country.

By the late 1950s, things had changed. This was a period in the country's history that would eventually lead to independence on 30 June 1960. Against this background of unrest, and with my mother pregnant with her first child, my parents decided to return to Belgium. I was born in Brussels in 1959, but I like to say I was made in the Congo. Throughout my youth, I absorbed my grandfather's inspiring stories about his challenges in central Africa. He was a pioneer, and his example made me determined to be a pioneer in my own way. That spirit he passed down to me was far better than anything he could have left me in a will.

From the fringe to the West End

When I arrived in London on a cold day in early 1985, I slept the first night in my car. The next day I was put up at the Alliance Française, the French cultural centre. Soon I found a room in a house owned by a 92-year-old lady who charged me £52 a week for half-board. Although I cannot honestly praise her cooking, my landlady was extremely helpful in other ways. I discovered that, over the years, she had accumulated a treasure trove of vintage books and leather luggage, which were cluttering up her loft and gathering a thick coat of dust. She hadn't been up there for years. By now, I had been in London long enough to have been drawn into the magic of the markets in Camden and Portobello Road, and I sensed an opportunity. When I asked whether I could empty her loft of bric-a-brac for a split of the profits, she was only too happy to agree.

This became my first independent business venture: selling a suitcase. I found a couple of guys who had an antiques stand in a street off Portobello Road, and I brought them the vintage books and leather cases that I had polished assiduously in the evenings after my English classes in Highgate. This was fun. In partnership with my new Rasta friends, I was living the street trader experience and learning to integrate into one of the world's most multicultural cities. For the first time in my life, I had my own money – albeit not much. But there was enough for me to reward myself with a luxury: a ticket to watch Tottenham Hotspurs playing at home. I loved the atmosphere in football stadiums, but I'd never heard anything like the passion and singing at White Hart Lane.

My market trader life and my English classes didn't last long. After a month or so, I became frustrated at the speed of my progress, and had had enough of learning the language in an academic setting. I figured it would make more sense to learn by offering my services in a professional environment – to take the full immersion approach. But where should I start?

London's law firms clearly needed to know I was in town! After all, I had grafted for a degree in law! But I quickly learned another lesson: London was not Liège. This was a city of 10 million people, not 300,000, and it had a *lot* of law firms. Not to be daunted, I decided to open the Yellow Pages at L and start calling law firms and asking for their addresses. This was tedious, but not half as tedious as handwriting my rather skeletal CV countless times. I felt like I was throwing darts at a dartboard with no idea of the rules of the game. But I was committed and determined. I was asking for an opportunity; I was confident I could take it from there.

I very soon caught a lucky break; even if it was 'lucky' in the Gary Player sense of the word. Remember the legendary South African golfer's famous line? 'It's funny, but the harder I practise the luckier I seem to get' – a quote that resonates with me to this day. He meant, of course, that if you put in the hard yards, you are more likely to get the results you want. In my painstaking quest for an interview, I really had put in the work – so I was in the right place to be able to make the most of the good fortune I received.

One of my CVs found its way to Nabarro Nathanson, at the time one of the most reputable law firms in the country. A hugely respected firm, it would grow to have more than 400 lawyers in six offices before it was absorbed in the largest ever merger in the UK legal sector. To put things in perspective, the biggest firm in my hometown had four partners at the time. Incredibly, the company offered me an interview.

You can imagine my trepidation and excitement. I was on my way to the first interview of my life, hardly able to speak English, but absolutely determined to make the most of this opportunity. I dressed as smartly as I could afford and borrowed a pair of glasses to give me a more serious and academic look. Filled with positivity, in the late evening of January 1985 I was welcomed by one of the senior partners. He didn't waste time with small talk. He began by asking what I could do for them. I replied that I was keen to learn English, to understand common law and to have the opportunity to work in his environment. I told him I was so keen for a chance that I was offering my services for free. I would do any type of job from filing to delivering mail to being the tea boy. If I proved inefficient at any of these things, I said with a smile, I would even clean the office after hours.

I guess he liked my ballsy approach and sensed my determination to do whatever it took to get my foot in the door. Or maybe it was because I was a French speaker. Whatever his actual thought process was, for me it was bingo! I could start the next Monday. What was all this fuss about getting a job? The first dart I threw: bullseye! And, despite my offer to work for nothing, it came with a salary of £50 a week. That didn't even cover my rent, but it didn't matter to me. Of course, I now know how lucky I was. Yes, I was ballsy, brave and determined, but many people are all of those things and still don't catch the breaks. I highly doubt that the hiring process in a large law firm would work the same way now. Nevertheless, at the time I felt amazing. Nothing was going to stop me now! I was on a roll – I was on the ladder.

I arrived in the office on my first day looking like a bridegroom fitted by a Jermyn Street tailor. I will never forget the feeling of pride with which I was infused. It was certainly an upgrade from my street trader garb in the Portobello Road. This was my big break: I was working for a prestigious law firm! I informed my parents of my achievement and I got back into my dad's good books by stressing that the heights I had reached were the result of my adventurous international outlook. I picked up some sheets of the firm's letterheaded paper and wrote to all my fellow law student friends to share my pride. The office was surrounded by shops selling authentic British luxury goods so, in what was to become the habit of a lifetime, I decided to reward myself again for having achieved something and bought an Alfred Dunhill umbrella. It was stolen a week later.

Opportunity knocks

They say lightning never strikes twice, but in my experience luck certainly can. I took every opportunity to make friends with everyone at

Nabarro Nathanson, from the post room staff to the lawyers and senior management. This was London, so that naturally included drinks in the pub after work. A few weeks after joining, I discovered how productive this could be.

One evening in the pub, my new boss asked whether I could help on a private matter. It involved a bailiff who had over-enthusiastically seized his daughter's furniture from an apartment in Antwerp.

'Consider it done, sir,' I responded immediately. Afterwards, I scratched my head, wondering exactly how I could keep my promise. Having slept on it, an answer came to me. I called Pascal, a university friend and former flatmate who was working in a law firm in Antwerp. I explained the situation, emphasizing that this was a make-or-break moment for my career and that his help was exceptionally important. He would inquire about the matter and we would reconvene. Being the very efficient guy he is, Pascal got on the case and sorted it out by himself. The situation was a profound misunderstanding between the bailiff and the tenant.

From London, with the partner beside me, I organized a 'conference call' with Pascal. Using our respective languages, Pascal and I demystified the situation. Through Pascal, I had helped to unblock the problem. The appreciative partner asked me whether there was anything he could do to thank me. 'Yes indeed, sir,' I said, feeling as though I were polishing the Genie's lamp.

To understand why I felt that way, there are two things I need to explain: my love of sport and my admiration for a certain Mark H. McCormack.

I am an avid sportsman. I play, I watch, I read, I consume sport. The love of competition is in my blood. My boarding school, Collège du Christ Roi, which I attended from the ages of 10 to 13, really valued sport and had fantastic facilities. (That's the reason I went there, to be honest.) I was a goalkeeper, the fastest swimmer in my county and played tennis whenever I could. I excelled at high jump and played every team sport possible, winning countless medals. However, my best performances were definitely taking place outside the classroom!

I was from the generation of cyclist Eddy Merckx, my hero and the most famous Belgian of all time. My bedroom was covered with posters of Joël Robert and Giacomo Agostini, both motor-cycling world champions multiple times over. I would spend my weekends faffing around on my 50cc motocross bike. I was essentially an adrenaline junkie and sport provided the shot.

Right at that time, I was reading the book *What They Don't Teach You at Harvard Business School*, which had become my bible. It was written by McCormack, the American visionary and father of the sports business who founded the International Management Group (IMG).

McCormack had trained as a lawyer and was initially a sports agent. He started his firm by representing the three iconic golf champions: Arnold Palmer, Gary Player and Jack Nicklaus. He then expanded by signing the most famous athletes and celebrities of the time: French alpine skier and Olympic champion Jean-Claude Killy, three-times Formula One drivers' champion Sir Jackie Stewart and, later, tennis stars Björn Borg, Andre Agassi, Rafael Nadal and Roger Federer, and golfing superstar Tiger Woods, to name but a few. This book had opened my eyes and given me the appetite to forge a career in this world.

By an incredible coincidence, I learned that McCormack was a client of Nabarro Nathanson, the very firm where I had pitched up as an intern. (I discovered this through my natural inquisitiveness about client files – or what some might call being nosy.)

Back to the partner, the Genie's lamp and me. Even though I had been at the firm no time at all, I asked him – with the utmost respect – whether he could write a letter of recommendation to Mark McCormack.

Everybody wanted to work for IMG and the firm was inundated with unsolicited applications. This was a lot to ask. But he assured me that he would be delighted to write a few words on my behalf.

An interview at IMG. In less than two weeks, my academic inferiority complex had been brushed aside. I had walked into one of the most respected law firms in the United Kingdom and had bounced from that onto the doorstep of the business that was everything I could have dreamed of.

More determined than ever, I psyched myself up to make the most of this once-in-a-lifetime opportunity. I felt like a pilgrim heading to Rome for an audience with the Pope. It was more than a dream come true; it surpassed my wildest expectations. I was 24 years old and tomorrow I would be knocking on the door of the world's most famous sports management organization. Me – someone who had been called 'the little f***ing Belgian' (a nickname, by the way, which stuck right to the end of my career) – parachuted in from nowhere, still searching for words in my broken English. I knew I could not mess it up. That train was never going to stop at the station again.

Mastering the stress, I was once again determined to seize my chance, to sell myself the best I could. This was me, my passion, my destiny. I walked into the interview knowing failure was not an option.

It was 26 February 1985 when I pushed open the imposing varnished white door of the IMG

European headquarters on Queen Anne Street. I had two interviews set up, one with Mark Lawson, the head of legal, and one with John Webber, the chief financial officer.

On the desk of my first interview, I spotted the letter of recommendation from Nabarro Nathanson, complete with some handwritten notes which appeared to say, 'Let's see this guy.' It was signed 'Ian'.

Ian Todd was a lawyer and former British Olympic skier who had been at IMG since 1971. He was one of McCormack's top three lieutenants, the head of the European business, and would become my boss. Ian was also, and still is, my mentor. We would go on to enjoy over 30 years of friendship.

The opening question was hardly a surprise: 'What can you do for us?' My heart was thumping, cold sweat was running down my back. But I tried to stay composed and cool, respectful but engaged.

Not wanting to change a winning formula, I adopted the same approach I had for the interview at Nabarro Nathanson.

'This is my passion,' I explained. 'I would really love to work for you.'

I told them they could pay me only when I bought them deals and made money for the company. I was striking a chord, so I pushed on. I spoke confidently about my relationships with international companies within the sports industry – companies like Donnay, the tennis equipment manufacturer, beer company Stella Artois and others, like Côte d'Or and Godiva (both of which make the best Belgian chocolates, by the way!). Maybe I got carried away and exaggerated a little about how well I knew these companies, but I was confident that hiring me – a young guy full of hope and determination – was a win–win situation. They must have felt the same way, as I was offered an internship on the spot. In fact, I was determined not to leave the office until the proposal had been confirmed and then I offered to start immediately. I couldn't wait to get going!

In that moment, I was taken back to that ferry crossing and Brel's words. I had left my personal Vilvoorde. And to make things a little more magical, it was my 25th birthday.

Rise to stardom

That was my first real job, and I stayed at the company for the next 30 years. From an internship in the legal department, I quickly migrated to a commercial role – it suited me better than legal. I was making myself known, available and helpful wherever possible. The post room became my canteen, and a platform to perfect my English. I did all the jobs I could to propel my career, and I couldn't believe how lucky I was that I was being paid to do things that most people only dream of doing. I was using my language skills to sell sponsorships for French athletes. I coordinated a communications campaign with soft drink Gini for Procter and Gamble. I got involved with the sponsorship programme of the Kouros Yves Saint Laurent aftershave brand for the Mercedes endurance racing team. I joined the European sponsorship sales force in charge of the Benelux territories.

In 1987, I moved to Paris and became part of the organizing committee's office for the 1992 Olympic Winter Games in Albertville, France. Ian had sent me to the Games in Calgary in Canada in 1988 to study how the commercial programme was handled. I brought that knowledge to bear in my consulting role for Jean-Claude Killy and Michel Barnier, the two co-presidents of the 1992 Games.

I've always loved the Olympics, especially the magic of the Opening and Closing Ceremonies. To me, they are the greatest show on earth, where everything – friendship, humanity, performance, athletes, management, media, art – comes together. In between, there are great moments of sport, for sure – but those ceremonies are what really stick in my mind.

After that, I opened an IMG office in Brussels. Next, I took my first steps into the booming pay-TV industry by helping to broker a deal in Asia between Rupert Murdoch's Star TV and the Chinese Football Association. Later, I became involved in the newly created media division, where I would go on to become head of rights sales for Europe, then head of sales worldwide. In the process, I created a media entertainment business. I lived through two takeovers, the first being when McCormack passed away in 2003 and

Teddy Forstmann, from Forstmann Little, bought IMG for US$750 million. The second, 10 years later, was the deal with WME. In the process, I became the president of IMG Events & Media, the world's largest independent producer and distributor of sports programming. Later, I became chairman.

I still pinch myself when I remember that first interview at IMG. A large helping of luck and being in the right place at the right time were at play, for sure – but I do think you create your own opportunities too. I was determined to take my chance, and I found the resources, inspiration and mental strength to put myself in a favourable position.

There has never been a dull moment serving three pioneers, rainmakers and game changers: Mark McCormack, Ted Forstmann and Ari Emanuel.

McCormack represented the true spirit of constant innovation and anticipation. He inspired me to work hard, to develop creative thinking and to excel at serving clients. It was a privilege to work for the founder of the sports marketing industry.

Forstmann had a very different style and personality. He was arguably the inventor of the modern private equity business, so he taught me how to create wealth. He took me under his wing and I discovered the world of the super-rich: the private jets, yachting holidays, casinos and auction houses.

Emanuel was a mesmerizing entrepreneur, a Hollywood uber agent, compulsively driven with an insatiable appetite for growth. Mad on the outside but profoundly human and emotional on the inside.

I have had the most mind-blowing and adventurous journey that I could ever have imagined. I have learned and progressed, often through my mistakes. I was certainly not afraid to take risks on my way to developing my expertise. Every year on my birthday, I engage in some serious self-reflection. I think about what it took for me to seize the opportunities that have come my way during my career: passion and determination. Even today, as I pursue new business and philanthropic projects, they remain key ingredients in the way I live my life.

From intern to chairman, the years in between have been an epic journey, fuelled by my enduring belief: where there's a will, there's a way. Don't be afraid to take to the stage!

CHAPTER 2

WHO ARE YOU?

During my 30-year career at IMG, I hired a lot of people. At the beginning of every interview, I would ask, 'Who are you? Why should I hire you?'

Who are you? It may seem like the simplest of questions – perhaps even a little banal. But believe me, finding the answer is fundamental to your prospects in life. Are you an artist, a follower, a rebel, a salesperson, a rainmaker, a philosopher, a doer, a transformer? Perhaps you are an unconventional thinker, an administrator, a researcher, a leader or someone who strives to help others? The key to your identity is understanding what motivates you – in other words, it's about finding your passion in life.

For those who struggled to define their identity and who showed no passion, it would be a very short interview. But for those who could, I would go on to ask about the other qualities – their determination, their ambition, their X-factor – that would make them suitable for the job. The number of people who apply for jobs and position themselves purely on exam results, or on academic achievements, is astonishing to me. Whatever exam results or work history you *can* show, it is most valuable when it is used as evidence of an identity built on passion.

These two questions – Who are you? What is your passion? – are interlinked. In some respects, you could say they are two parts of the same question. We are all multi-faceted individuals, and discovering who we are is the most important building block for the rest of our lives. You are so much more than the details in your passport; these are things that were decided for you and were never under your control.

Deciding who we really are can be a challenge. Some stumble upon the answer early, others only gradually, through the experiences on their journey. But there are those who never find the answer because they never take the trouble to seek it. In fact, experience has taught me that what is unacceptable in someone is not knowing who they are. You simply cannot go through life ignorant of your real self. You cannot afford to be unaware of what drives you, what you fear, where you excel and where you are challenged. You have to understand your ability to relate, to inspire, to guide or to lead.

It is inconceivable that a musician does not love creating sounds, an athlete does not enjoy competition, an actor does not want to play with the audience's emotions, an entrepreneur does not get excited about creating new businesses, a salesperson does not enjoy over-delivering, an accountant is not at home with numbers and a poet is not in love with words. They have more chance of achieving extraordinary results if they are in the groove of their passion and fuelled by the adrenaline of living what they love.

Only by finding your passion and discovering who you really are will you be in harmony with yourself. When you are working with your passion, you will find endless energy. You will perform with a level of authenticity because you are in a role that reflects your personality, your DNA, what you are born with. This does not guarantee that your journey will end in success, but it is a hell of a ticket to start the ride!

Schools do not train stars

We are all born with talents, some of which we may not be aware of or may not immediately discover in ourselves. Time, opportunity and experience tend to bring out these talents and lead to self-discovery. As long as we are allowed to find our true identity and individual passion, we are able to deliver, achieve and create – often much more than we could ever have imagined. The key factor here, of course, is opportunity – and it deeply concerns me that we still live in a world in which too much of society, from the education system onwards, is structured in a way that stifles opportunity and represses the realization of potential.

Too often we have limited perceptions of what we can do and what we can achieve. Perhaps we were born in the wrong place at the wrong time, or in the wrong community, and only discover that we have powerful imaginations, senses of anticipation or physical, mental and intellectual skills later in life. The struggle to find these skills and talents within ourselves is exacerbated by the conventions and demands of the society in which we grow up, a society that – even in the third decade of the twenty-first century – tends to repress the discovery and development of talent. That repression is, perhaps unintentionally, delivered through a rigid and conservative education system, a one-dimensional culture and even parents who are unable to understand their kids' individuality because of their own limited experience of life and lack of self-awareness.

Society is designed to support conformity, and most of us naturally feel more comfortable following the crowd than pursuing our instincts. Throughout our education, we are put under pressure to deliver good results; kids are evaluated on standardized tests and institutes place them in boxes and measure them against the law of the average. All this is totally counterproductive to the concept of motivation; it is a massive barrier to the inner search to discover who we are and to find our passion.

I am not writing off education and the massive benefits it brings to societies worldwide, of course: quite the opposite. I rejoice in a global society which has provided access to schools and education and driven unprecedented progress over the last few decades. I am saying, though, that standard education across the world is not entirely fit for purpose. The current system is too often narrow and dull. The methods used to judge students are inadequate, because they fail to find true genius and are too rigid to allow students to find it themselves.

Education should be about personalization, not standardization. Its aim should be to discover and stimulate talent, even when it is not immediately obvious, and to push students beyond their comfort zones to naturally discover their passions. Benjamin Franklin had no formal education, but he became a writer, a business strategist, an imaginative polymath, a scientist and, of course, an inventor. From electricity to bifocal glasses, from mapping the Gulf Stream to creating clean-burning stoves, he was prolific – a man of many passions. Everybody knows the legacy of Albert Einstein, but are you aware he played Mozart? Leonardo da Vinci had almost no schooling. Like Newton and many other creators, he was driven by sheer determination, by a passion for life, by research, curiosity, ambition.

Leonardo's ability to observe, imagine and create led him, among other things, to invent the parachute before planes existed. He produced plans for modern waterways. He designed war machines and backgrounds for theatres with the same enthusiasm. He was an artist, an engineer, a scientist, a humanist, a sculptor, a botanist, a painter, an anatomist and probably the world's greatest innovator. The *Mona Lisa* was the first augmented reality experience. I hate to think what he would have produced working for Fortnite! An illegitimate child, vegetarian, left-handed and gay – in the fifteenth century – da Vinci was unusual for his times in so many ways, and probably not the kind of person who would have scored high on standardized tests. Yet his relentless curiosity, defiance and will to experiment propelled him to become one of the greatest of all time.

How many potential da Vincis did not blossom? How many Newtons might there be without access to opportunities? How many potential Mozarts or Steve Jobs have not had the chance to reveal themselves? There are enough examples around us of people in the fields of sports, science, business, and the arts and humanities who should inspire and motivate us to do something special with the gift of life.

Look at how Impressionists and Surrealists broke out of the classic portrait school. They were ridiculed by the critics and the public at expo after expo, but they never compromised on what they believed in. They sacrificed everything in the belief their new way of seeing the world would one day be understood and their talent recognized. It took many decades, and they didn't all live to see it. Van Gogh sold only one painting during his lifetime. His *Portrait du Docteur Gachet* sold for US$75 million in 1990.

We all have extraordinary talents. They need to be stimulated and revealed. We need the audacity to believe in ourselves, to dive with confidence into the unknown.

Instead, society rewards conformism. Not enough people are encouraged to be rebels and live their true passions; it's hard to break out of the box, and everything around us is straining to keep that lid closed. There are so many examples of successful people who have made a difference in the world despite, rather than because of, their education. They survived an academic experience that suffocated their identity and shattered their confidence.

And it's not completely surprising. Let's face it, the modern world is changing so fast that it is difficult just to keep up, let alone be ahead of the curve. The education system is constantly playing catch-up; future generations will have many different types of career opportunities, and it is likely that the types of work they will do don't yet exist. The only thing we can predict about the future is that it will be different, and that the process of transformation will continue to accelerate. The pace of change means the key skill is the ability to successfully navigate uncharted waters, not to answer textbook questions.

I understand the frustration with an ill-fitting school system because I have experienced it.

Find the right stage for your talent

In the cultural and educational environment I was born into, I was something of a reject, and as a result I was ranked as a mediocre student until I started discovering myself, my passion and my identity. As a kid, I was thrown into a kind of academic championship of testing, scores and rankings. It was just the way things were, accepted by everybody, including my parents, who endorsed it and encouraged me to play the game. But not everybody can play by the rules of this game, and a dancer may not perform well on a singer's stage. I was among those who were measured by the wrong yardstick. Even as a child, I felt backed into a corner by the need to produce the right school results.

I was not jealous of my brainy colleagues who were successfully surfing the waves of examinations while I was drowning in my syllabus, lacking intellectual self-confidence and developing an inferiority complex. But I certainly was frustrated. And that frustration taught me an important lesson: I had to find my own path and search for my own routes to success.

I had a strange relationship with school. To say I was not passionate about life in the classroom is an understatement, yet I loved going to school because of the social environment. Early in my educational life, I was sent to boarding school; here, I was in my element among my peers. That I was expelled twice tells you something about my relationship with authority, but outside the classroom I revelled in the company of others. I came to understand that it was this environment that fostered my appetite for sociability, and it was among this varied group of characters that my identity began to be revealed. I found I was generally popular with my schoolmates and began to sense that I could be a creative leader. I enjoyed bringing friends together for various causes: challenges, missions, school trips, editing school newspapers and organizing fundraising events were among the kinds of activities I would engage in.

Given the opportunity to read out loud at school, I discovered I was comfortable in front of an audience, something that stood me in good stead both as a drummer in our schoolboy band and as a DJ. In fact, I often combined the two, taking my drum kit onstage when I was DJing and blasting away to add a little edge to some of the tracks I played. Naturally, I organized and promoted the gigs myself – there was no one else to do it.

So, despite school not being the best fit for me academically, I had the chance to thrive and discover myself in the social environment of school. Later, at university in Louvain la Neuve, this discovery continued in a place where the liberated atmosphere encouraged the idea that we could do whatever we put our minds to. For me, that involved organizing a 24-hour cycling event on campus; it was as much carnival as competition, and attracted teams, their highly decorated bikes and other cycling contraptions from all over the country. It was a great excuse for a party, and we didn't miss the opportunity. The event became so popular that it featured on the national TV news and we even had a visit from cycling legend Eddy Merckx.

As the head of the university's entertainments committee, I organized many different social events and competitions, a lot of which seemed to involve drinking! But there was a more serious side to the role. I launched a series of political debates and public speaking competitions which became known and respected way beyond the university, with politicians and celebrities often joining us as judges. These were the things that occupied my mind at university, much more than the learning I was 'supposed' to be doing, and it became clear that what I could achieve in my spare time was more important than my studies.

I see now that this was when and how I began to discover my identity and my passion, and when I realized I was going to make a living out of entertainment. In essence, I discovered I was a natural promoter, thriving on excess, pushing everything to the limits. I was an adventurer who enjoyed life beyond the beaten track.

I think my teachers were right when they said I had little academic intelligence and that I was no good at solving casebook problems. I was certainly neither confident nor motivated (one probably goes with the other) by academic challenges. On the other hand, I had found among my peers an environment where I could exercise my avid curiosity and desire to get involved with creative thinking, to follow my gut feelings and voice practical suggestions in exciting and unusual contexts.

Gather your cast and crew

So where do you find your passion? I found mine at school and university – albeit not through my studies – but the simple answer is that you can find your passion within you at any time, so long as you have the ambition to do so. And remember that life is no more a monologue than it is a dress rehearsal; discovering your passion is a process that will involve the people you are close to, your friends and your parents. You can draw inspiration from the books you read, the TV documentaries you watch, the mentors you encounter and, hopefully, the help of some exceptional teachers who are equally passionate. Or you can simply follow your dreams – those places your mind takes you to whether you like it or not.

I vividly remember some of my teachers, those who saw in me talents of which I was unaware. Their words of encouragement and consideration still resonate with me today, much more than the subjects studied in their classes. I found they transmitted their own energy to me and, most importantly, empowered me to take brave steps.

Friends can be powerful influencers too. We tend to identify or distance ourselves from 'group attitudes'. The way our senior peers behave – good or bad – as well as the way they look, the way they speak, the way they dress, how they perform or lead all stimulate us in one way or another. Some we want to emulate, others we will naturally react against and do whatever it takes *not* to be like them. Either way, positive or negative, they can help shape us.

On many occasions I have been inspired by the achievers within my community. I have been motivated by their passion, and my sense of competition has been sparked – I wanted to prove myself equal to the company of those I admired.

At a later stage in life, I discovered many passions through the influence of a whole range of mentors. Some people are inspiring because of what they have achieved, and others because of their charisma, or the way they went from zero to hero and broke the rules all the way. How can you not be encouraged to be an achiever when you look at the journeys of scientists Stephen Hawking and Albert Einstein? How can you fail to be inspired by activists such as Malala Yousafzai and Nelson Mandela, or the personal journey of Michelle Obama? These were all people whose remarkable lives touched and influenced my own through the pages of biographies.

I have always loved reading biographies, and I have been heavily influenced by the lives of some of the awesome individuals I have studied. The first biography I read was that of Joël Robert, the Belgian motocross world champion who dominated the 250cc class from the 1960s to the 1970s. I was 12. At school, when they asked us to talk about a great person, the others were talking about Napoleon and other famous historical figures. I talked about Joël Robert. Still now, I devour biographies and the lessons of others' lives. For my 60th birthday, I was presented with a two-volume autobiography by the great French skier and businessman Jean-Claude Killy, with whom I had worked on the 1992 Olympic Winter Games in Albertville. The first volume focuses on Killy the athlete, the second on his business life. Both are equally fascinating.

But it doesn't take an internationally recognized high achiever to influence a life. It can be the people you meet or those you work with. They are the people who gave you a chance in life, who gave you some good advice, who gave you opportunities to be yourself, to be entrepreneurial, to take risks, and who supported you in your desire to achieve your own goals. On a personal level, I certainly owe a tremendous amount to a handful of key people to whom I will forever be grateful.

But while these positive influences are hugely important, you will also find your passion as a reaction to negative influences. I had an uneasy relationship with my father; we had very different views of the world, and his ambitions for me didn't match my own. I wanted to prove him wrong by going in the opposite direction and showing not only him, but myself, that my success would be built far away from home. As discussed in Chapter 1, the day I finally received my diploma, I set sail and never came back.

Our discovery of our own passions can be shaped by the influence of others, and the cast and crew around you are vital. But nobody is going to do the work for you. Finding your passions is a self-help exercise. A friend, a book, a movie, a conversation, a celebrity, a coach, a teacher, a boss or any combination of circumstances can ignite sparks, but the explosion is within you. My advice is not to become indoctrinated by a system designed for the masses rather than individuals. Find out who you are, what you like and what you are good at; be aware that you have talents, regardless of what people may tell you. Passion and motivation are constants in the equation for success.

When you find your passions, your life will take on a new dimension. You will wake up with a fresh perspective and a real sense of purpose. Without that, you may as well stay in bed! Discovering and living your passions does not mean you have acquired some sort of Golden Ticket to a successful and fulfilling life, but until you do life will be an uphill struggle and ultimately far less rewarding in every way. The journey can be a zigzag rather than a straight line; it's a process, and some things only start to fully make sense retrospectively.

As Mark Twain said, 'The two most important days in your life are the day you are born and the day you find out why.'

Looking back, I can see it emerging at university but even before that: being in a band, being a DJ, organizing school trips, organizing photography exhibitions, being head of class. This was all before I was 18. At the time, I didn't see myself as a leader, but I was an enthusiast demonstrating leadership.

There are also those light-bulb moments. Reading Mark McCormack's book was one of those. While I was reading it, I was thinking, 'That's going to be my environment; he's going to be my boss.'

What is your passion? It's inside you. Find it. It's an act of discovery.

CHAPTER 3

THINK POSITIVE: FACE BOOS OR APPLAUSE WITH A SMILE

Rather than a pessimist, an optimist or a realist, I would describe myself as a 'possibilist'. I'm not unrealistically hopeful, nor am I down-in-the-dumps negative, but I believe in *possibility*. Put it like this: I have a natural tendency to believe I have more chance of succeeding than of failing, and that achievement is within my reach. I try to maintain a positive temperament overall. I believe that such a state of mind can trigger a series of benefits, such as boosting self-confidence, stimulating creativity and even helping you create your own luck. It increases productivity. It releases adrenaline, which creates a positive dynamic when you're under pressure. Such energy will be a great ally in your career. It will make you more popular with your peers. And it will bring inner happiness in your journey.

Were you born a 'possibilist'? Is it part of your DNA? I believe it comes naturally to certain individuals, but it can also be cultivated and developed over time. I don't think anyone is born a pessimist, but if that's your natural state of mind, self-motivation may be harder for you. I am convinced, though, that you are still capable of marshalling your feelings to boost your creativity, to improve your performance or develop a skill.

This takes me back to my sociology exam in June 1977. My professor was Léo Moulin, who had written a book on sociology called *Les Socialisations: Société, État, Parti* two years earlier. He threw me a question regarding the *inné* versus the *acquis* – essentially, nature versus nurture. I attacked the ball before it bounced and, abandoning academic theory, embarked on a highly personal and passionate speech that really engaged him. This was the only exam I passed at the first attempt.

More than four decades later, my thoughts on the matter have evolved, but the gist remains largely the same. Regardless of where you were born, what you were told and what is written in your genes, if you believe that where there is a will there is a way, then I have no doubt that there is a good chance your journey will be more successful and more rewarding. I genuinely believe you can look at the road that has been mapped out for you and choose a different path. Don't listen to people who tell you that you have no talent just because they can't see it, and don't believe that the obstacles you may face are insurmountable. With determination and positive thinking – a possibilist mentality – you can be on your way to being the artisan building your own future.

The right lighting can make all the difference

In February 1991, I was the organizer of an official ATP tennis tournament at the Forest National arena in Brussels, the venue of choice in Belgium for all the top rock bands, from the Rolling Stones to Supertramp. The date of the event slotted perfectly into the international tennis tour calendar, and we attracted 14 out of the top 15 players in the world at the time.

The Brussels Hilton housed a 'who's who' of tennis greats: Jim Courier, John McEnroe, Boris Becker, Ivan Lendl and the long-haired superstar Andre Agassi, over from Las Vegas, continually surrounded by his herd of adoring fans. Agassi was the ambassador of the Donnay tennis racquet, which was manufactured in Belgium's Ardennes region, and we had brought in Donnay to be the title sponsor of the event, the Donnay Indoor Championships.

There were more sponsors and VIPs too: DHL, which had its world headquarters in the Belgian capital, was also the sponsor of Jim Courier, who had just become world number one. The company had invited its most important clients. Car company Renault was there as the official transport partner of the event, along with select car dealers. French water company Perrier had a series of celebrities lined up to attend, such as Eddy Merckx, who did the competition draw. The Italo-Belgian singer Salvatore Adamo brought his family. Argentinian President Carlos Menem, who was making a diplomatic visit to Brussels, was due to make an appearance. All would be mingling with ministers and other dignitaries, keen to be seen with the local jet set.

There was a real buzz. Brussels had become the focal point of Europe. TV and radio stations, newspapers and magazines everywhere were talking about this event. A few months before, I had opened an IMG office in Brussels, and this was the first event we had organized. We wanted to make this tournament special and glamorous, and we pushed ourselves to be innovative: we had a luxurious outdoor hospitality tent built in the arena car park to provide first-class entertainment for the VIP guests of our sponsors. Belgium's national broadcaster, RTBF, had deployed its production infrastructure for the event, which would be broadcast live globally.

The excitement was palpable. Then, two days before the event was due to begin, while all the world's greatest tennis players were out on the courts practising, disaster struck. Our vaguely worded rental agreement for the arena did not specify that we could use the spaces around the arena itself. A giant retail chain that had a store on the same site launched a compensation claim for our use of the car park. Then council officials questioned the safety of our hastily built infrastructure. On top of that, the exclusive arena caterers threatened a compensation claim, unhappy that we had arranged an haute cuisine restaurant outside for our VIPs. The venue owners, the caterers, the local general store, the city council, our architects and the security officers were all at loggerheads, all with their respective lawyers pouring petrol on the fire. It was the perfect storm. And there was less than 48 hours to go.

For someone with limited experience, like me, it was an incredibly stressful situation. I could not see a viable solution. I decided to bring all the parties together in one room, out of the public's gaze, to thrash it all out, but after a couple of hours of legal tit-for-tat, the situation was worse. With provocative attitudes and aggressive egos, it was becoming explosive.

I paused and took a deep breath. What I needed was for everyone to see the situation in a different light. I decided to launch a last-ditch appeal to try to find a positive attitude. 'Come on guys,' I launched in, 'we all have more to lose than to gain here. We are better people than this situation reflects. Let's park our differences and egos for a minute and see if we can rise above this dark cloud. Failing to do so will mean we have to face the press and make a joint statement cancelling this prestigious event. This would lead to international ridicule for everyone involved.'

It wasn't some moment of genius or an inspiring speech on my part – just a simple plea and reminder of the potential fallout – but the mood changed almost instantly. Looking at things in a new, more positive light – what we all had to gain from working together – meant that, slowly but surely, the weapons were laid down. The negative had turned into a positive. Not only did we all agree to compromise, but the reverse dynamic came into effect: everyone started to throw in some creative thinking of their own, suggesting solutions instead of hurling objections.

The day of the competition, after the first ball was served, everyone who had been fighting tooth and nail in that room was now raising a glass with each other in the VIP area. They all became friends. And naturally, everyone claimed the credit for solving the mess! The strange thing was that, in the end, little had changed materially. There was no brilliant intervention by a lawyer, no particular concession or compromise that unblocked the situation. It was simply that a positive mood had replaced a negative one. Clearing the air in that room – being a possibilist and changing the light – had allowed the magic to happen.

During ups and downs with difficult situations in my career, the Donnay Indoor Championships have often come to mind. Taking major issues, breaking them up into smaller problems and having a positive mindset were key ingredients in making a success of an apparently intractable situation. This story is an example of how you can arm yourself with the feeling of being a possibilist to solve challenging situations. To me, it was a defining moment where the line between success and failure was so fine that only the magic of positive belief could push the ball to one side of the net or the other.

Find positivity in those around you

It's not just my own attitude I try to keep focused on the positive. I love to surround myself with people who are 'solution finders' – those who believe they can shape their future and have a smile on their face while doing so. One such person who comes to mind is Bella Nokes.

Ten years after the ATP event, in 2001, I had helped establish a major distribution network, selling TV rights to broadcasters around the world. Coming from the United States, Mark McCormack, the founder and chairman of IMG, had never been naturally drawn to football – but you can't really be in international sports marketing without being in football. Football is the number one sport in the world, but it was the most challenging business to operate. The culture of deal-making didn't fit with our school of sports management; at the time, football was characterized by some dubious trading practices and governed by unwritten rules. Things have changed over the last decade, and governing bodies such as FIFA and UEFA have done important work in ensuring that the commercial side of the game is now transparent and clean. However, enough has been written about this subject to be able to say, without any great controversy, that at that time football had become a dirty business in some respects. There were far too many grey areas.

Bella Nokes had joined me as my deputy head of sales. From the outset, I could see that she was in control of things: she had a pacifying influence on those around her, including me. She never panicked, never threw her toys out of the pram, no matter how bad things got. She always knew there was a solution. Bella is the definition of a positive thinker – and unflappable to boot. I asked her if she would dive in the deep end and help me with the serious challenge that being mired deep in the football business was creating for us. Piece by piece, step by step, she untangled this major ball of knots. We ruffled a few feathers, lost a bit of money, terminated a few dodgy deals, reached compromises here and there, and fired many people. But, thanks to her, we cleared the mess. We rebuilt new foundations on a more transparent footing to bring the football division in line with our rugby, golf, tennis and motorsports divisions.

When faced with a ball of knots, some people lose their patience and make a bad situation worse. But others will start with one thread, then another, and then another, and slowly unpick the knot. I observed and deliberately learned from Bella's example. Later, when colleagues would come to me with a long list of seemingly intractable problems I would say, 'Let's look at them separately. Okay, we can solve this one. Once we solve this one, that one will look less of an issue.' When you have tackled two or three of the issues, you start to see that some of the others are minor. The work may be hard, but having a positive attitude gets you through.

I tend to put as much distance as possible between myself and the scaremongers, the defeatists, the naysayers, the pessimists, those who only want to cover their own backsides. I'm sure you've met them: colleagues who always see the worst-case scenario and want to create an email chain so there is a record if things go wrong. This kind of attitude stymies and stalls instead of energizing and flowing – it kills innovation because it fears innovation. As I see it, this kind of doom-mongering spreads bad luck like a contagion.

Winston Churchill put it perfectly when he said, 'A pessimist sees the difficulty in every opportunity; an optimist sees the opportunity in every difficulty.'

If you want to have a dynamic spirit in your organization and among your colleagues, find people who have this positive thinking attitude, and those who live their lives in pursuit of fun and happiness. And then lead by example.

Sport's unscripted drama inspires

If you need examples of how positive thinking can create miracles, look no further than sport. The history of sport is *full* of examples of athletes and teams that pushed themselves beyond what they thought were their limits, underdogs who refused to lie down, teams that snatched victory from the jaws of defeat, players and teams that made comebacks literally nobody – apart from them – believed were possible. The unforgettable moments in sport are proof of what you can achieve with a possibilist mentality. That's what creates heroes.

I was privileged to be in Chicago for the 39th Ryder Cup in 2012, better known as the 'Miracle of Medinah' after the name of the golf club in Chicago, Illinois where the event was held. Europe, the titleholders, were in an impossible situation, needing 8.5 points to win going into the final day. To retain the cup, Martin Kaymer had to sink a five-foot putt on the 18th green. The German player's nerves must have been at breaking point, but *unbelievably* he sank the putt. Europe went on to win the final game and win the cup outright. Nothing is impossible or out of reach when you believe in magic!

Here's another one: if you follow football, you will probably never forget the night Manchester United scored two goals in injury time to take the UEFA Champions League out of the hands of Bayern Munich. The Bayern winner's ribbons had already been attached to the handles of the iconic trophy, but United's players simply refused to lose.

And another. The Clint Eastwood film *Invictus*, with Matt Damon as François Pienaar, the captain of the South African rugby team, and Morgan Freeman as Nelson Mandela, is one of my favourites. It tells the inspiring story of how the newly elected president of South Africa united the country to support the national team. Against the background of a nation still coming to terms with the wounds of apartheid, expectations for the South African team – the Springboks – were low at the 1995 World Cup, despite the country being the competition host. Against all the odds, South Africa defeated the mighty All Blacks of New Zealand 15 to 12 to lift the Web Ellis Cup, presented to Pienaar by Mandela.

Mandela gave Pienaar something else: the poem 'Invictus' – Latin for unconquerable – which he had had on the wall of his prison cell and would recite to the other prisoners on Robben Island, one of three prisons where he spent nearly 30 years of his life. The poem ends with the words, 'I am the master of my fate; I am the captain of my soul.'

The common denominator in these sporting moments is people who collectively or individually believed in themselves – truly *believed* that they could make miracles happen. You may not be performing on an international stage in front of thousands of spectators, but you too can be elevated by the power of self-belief. You too will experience moments of profound achievement. What is certain is that no one will believe in you if you do not first believe in yourself.

Like anybody, you will probably fall and fail many times. But the right state of mind will not only help you to pick yourself up; it will teach you to learn from your mistakes and try again, to formulate a new equation to reach your goal. In the face of failure, a pessimist will regret having even tried in the first place. When you accept a crisis or take on what seems to be an unsurmountable challenge, the best way forward is to switch your mind into being an adventurer. Success is a poor teacher, but adversity, struggle, mistakes and failures make you stronger. They build your strength and your expertise, and help you develop confidence. Passion, determination and hard work will fuel your creativity and sense of innovation. They will drive you to succeed and will trigger contentment. Focusing on what will work, rather than being deterred or scared about what could go wrong, will increase your chances of success and make the journey more exciting. Being a possibilist is like a form of super intelligence – and in fact it becomes infectious within your community. Your colleagues, friends, boss, subordinates, partners, employees – whoever is in your environment – will support you, respect you and want to work with you. Positive thinkers develop an aura. You, your team and your community will grow stronger, and together you will build your own success story, share your passions and create your adventure.

Of all our instincts, I think fear has the strongest influence on our behaviour. We are not born predators with big teeth or claws; we feel the need to protect ourselves against the elements. But a series of potential consequences occur when our behaviour is conditioned by fear: we will have little or no adventure; there will be a loss of confidence; we will show an aversion to taking risks; we will be conservative in our choices. This may keep us 'safe', but it will not drive success. Fortunately, we are also born with the most powerful and compact engine to combat and overcome such natural instincts: the brain. And with the evolution of the brain comes an array of weapons that will help you to release your potential. With this extraordinary control centre, you have the ability to inhibit the forces of negativity, to foster endless positive energy and to create a positive mindset. You are able to persist in the face of frustration, to motivate yourself, to control your impulses, to release endorphins, to regulate your mood, to control your stress, to turn a difficult situation or a challenging task into a successful outcome. People can sense when you are not confident, when you are insecure, when you are invaded by doubt, and they will distance themselves. By contrast, you will rally a crowd if you communicate the feeling that you believe in yourself and can generate a positive outcome whatever the situation.

I believe you have a choice: do you want to join the forces of success and contribute to a better world, or do you prefer to join the ranks of pessimists, suffocated by fear, and obstruct your own progress?

Do you want to live your life as a comedy or as a tragedy?

An honourable mention

I cannot finish this chapter without referring to the person who, for me, epitomizes the spirit of positivism. I have never heard my mother complain about anything. She went through cancer at an early age, she lost an eye in her sixties, she raised three strong-minded children with the same love and energy in the context of a tumultuous marital life, and she went through a painful divorce. She was raised under Nazi occupation. At the age of 10, she found herself in boarding schools in remote corners of Africa while her parents were away for long periods chasing business opportunities between Kinshasa and Lubumbashi. Despite having no advanced education, she first taught herself to become a real estate agent and later owned her own clothes shop.

During the COVID-19 pandemic that started in 2020, she spent 12 months confined, alone, in her apartment with only rare visits from family. Yet every Sunday when I call her, her opening line is: *'Tout va bien de mon côté et toi, quoi de neuf?'*

All good from my end. And you, what's new?

CHAPTER 4

FIND YOUR X-FACTOR

When I was about 17, my parents decided to have me tested by a psychologist. They were baffled as to why I was below average at school and constantly struggling, and so attempted to find an answer with a doctor. The office was poorly lit, a fitting environment for someone I found to be a grey, emotionless man. An air of sadness hung over the place. The ticking of an outsize wall clock filled the dead time. He took me through Q&As, made me do some drawings, showed me pictures and asked me what they meant, and analysed my handwriting. After hours of this soulless interaction, he produced a report supposed to direct me towards the future I was best suited to.

Here was a man who gave advice that could have a major impact on the future of a young person. This guy, with ill-fitting clothes, poor communication skills and zero charm, was going to decide the direction my life should take. If he was a master at shaping people's futures, how come he had done such a terrible job on himself? The report suggested that I should be reorientated towards 'more accessible' studies, whatever that meant. My parents refused to accept the 'results' and instead they duly organized extra work and tutoring that I was given during break times.

The more I was fed this regime, the worse I found it. I started to believe I had a weaker brain than my peers because I was not scoring well on standardized tests. My confidence was slowly disappearing down the drain. I was struggling with self-esteem, becoming depressed and disconnected. Yet, in spite of everything, I didn't feel like a loser. That's because I disagreed with what the establishment thought of me and refused to make that label a part of my identity. I was a young rebel loved by many of my peers. Yes, I was a bit of a troublemaker, but I had social traction. Some people liked my rebellious attitude. I was a good goalie, a fast swimmer and a confident flirt. I was doing readings at church and enjoying the 'stage' it gave me. I found happiness in unconventional ways. With one group of friends, that meant being a mechanic, discovering the art of motorcycle maintenance. With another, it meant cranking up our amps and blasting out some rock and roll. In the playground, I was a bit of a trader, wheeling and dealing to make extra pocket money. I started to push things a little further, importing goods from my trips abroad.

I ventured off the beaten track during weekends and holidays. From a chance meeting with a guy in Greece, I ended up being invited to his hometown in Bujumbura in Burundi, where he was organizing a motorcycling tour of the country, a four-day dirt-track event. I had no money and no bike, but had made up my mind I was going to take part; with my mother's blessing, I had packed a massive suitcase with unsold dresses from her clothing business. I didn't just sell them. I organized a fashion show for the local white ladies of the colonial expat community. The money I earned paid for the whole expedition.

It didn't happen overnight. There was no eureka moment. But over time I began to understand that I had something, and it was something that others could see in me. I didn't know exactly what it was. But whatever it was, it was my X-factor emerging.

Diversity and the X-factor

As humans, we are creative, adaptable, innovative and resilient. We have a unique ability to observe and learn, to combine experiences and knowledge to make decisions. Yet we are so often creatures of habit and tend to hang around with people like ourselves. We consume similar products, gather in digital bubbles. We like our comfort zone. In a society structured on sameness, how do you make yourself special? How do you become a valuable individual who makes a difference? How do you attract attention to yourself so you're hired instead of someone else? This is the paradox we face: we are required to conform to arbitrary standards, but will only shine through our individual qualities – the things that make us different, that make each of us unique.

Diversity is a deeply ingrained part of nature, and the human being is in a constant state of evolution. Humans survive and thrive because of *difference*, because of how we complement one another. Yet we inhabit a society that creates a pseudo homogeneity through arbitrary measures such as race, faith, political tendencies, gender, sexuality, income and IQ. I have always valued diversity as a key component of success. When I set up teams and partnerships, or collaborate with other organizations, I look for individuals who have something different. Someone with an edge, a street-smart person, a social animal, someone with emotional intelligence, multicultural savvy or a futuristic visionary with a talent for anticipation. I will never be excited by someone who is not exceptional at something; a winning team is not made of average players. But nor is a winning team made of clones of one great player.

From an early age, people begin to build their personality, discover their skills, abilities and passions, and establish what makes them different from others. Roy T. Bennett, the author of the book *The Light in the Heart: Inspirational Thoughts for Living Your Best Life*, could have been describing my own adolescence when he wrote,

'You are unique, you have different talents and abilities. You don't always have to follow in the footsteps of others and most importantly, you should always remind yourself that you don't have to do what everyone else is doing. You have the responsibility to develop the talents you are given.' I love what Bennett is saying here – not only is he exhorting us all to invest in ourselves, but he is reminding us that we *all* have something about us that makes us unique – which means we all have something valuable to bring to the stage. I strongly believe that you are the architect of your own uniqueness; the question is how you can design yourself in a way that allows you to be appreciated.

Use the wings you were born with. The bird born looking over the edge of its nest doesn't know it can fly, let alone glide and see the world from above. Find your wings and be adventurous! Innovate and commit to your individuality. Polish, develop, expand and thrive.

Challenge the algorithm that makes decisions for you.

Finding the X-factor in others

One of the things I take pride in is the creation of a team – lovingly called a team of mercenaries – who became the world's biggest sports media rights distributor. We were the partners, advisers and agents selling the broadcast rights of the most prestigious sports events, from Wimbledon, The British Open and the Rugby World Cup, to MotoGP, the US Open tennis and football's Premier League. When searching for exceptional executives who would inspire their own sales and management operations, there was no room for anything less than brilliant. I was looking for people with a distinct X-factor, a flame that could start a fire.

My search for key colleagues didn't follow a set format. Names and profiles rarely arrived via HR, and I didn't wade through piles of CVs. I was *certainly* not looking for grades or the 'right' university. I wanted to create a diverse team with complementary skills, so I had to be involved personally to see what they were like as people. Some were entrepreneurs or innovators, others were brilliant salespeople, and still others were extraordinary at coordinating a team or serving clients. Every single one of them was selected for their X-factor. We shared a sense of accountability, a team spirit, a will to win together and to deliver results beyond expectations. We were all passionate and determined, great at thinking outside the box. There was a strong mutual respect at every level. If I can claim a legacy, looking back at that period of my career, it is for having spotted unique talents and fostered a spirit of harmony: all for one and one for all. That team went from success to success for three decades. We were anticipating the business models of the future, and clients would congratulate us on having put together the A-Team. Many years later, we are still friends who remain in close contact, sharing our old war stories from the industry frontline with a sense of nostalgia.

Thinking back again to how I found this incredible team, interviews would rarely take place in a formal office setting. More often, I would have to fit them in on the road, at airports, bars or sports events. In November 2002, I was looking for someone to take over our Italian operation.

I had seen a few recommended candidates who seemed to have potential and I was ready to make up my mind and fly home to London. The night before I was due to leave, I made some time to meet a 29-year-old Italian guy who I'd been put in touch with via a casual conversation. Ioris Francini was helping Italian film studios to finance their films at the time, and on paper he didn't have the right profile or expertise for us. He didn't have a book of contacts in sport, didn't know everyone in the media. I could easily have written him off. We met at the Grand Plaza Hotel in central Rome. He dressed like an Italian; I was in jeans. He was on time; I was late. After a few beers and a chat about life, business and favourite places, we started to get on like a house on fire. I could see something in him – the elusive spark that convinced me he would work well as part of our team. We shook hands when the bar closed. This was the beginning of a professional collaboration that turned into lifelong friendship.

He got the job as head of sales in Italy. Within a few years, he became head of sales in Europe, then head of rights acquisition and sales worldwide, and finally the president of IMG Media. Sound familiar? Ioris took over my position when I left the company. Mark McCormack always said to hire people better than you: there will never be a better illustration of this principle. I had no set rules on how to judge character, brilliance or the ability to join the gang. The only thing the team all had in common was that they were able to demonstrate unique talents and capabilities. I wanted passion and determination, but that wasn't enough. I was searching for the magic, the extra light. I like to think that everyone I came across had an equal chance to pitch themselves, but it was the way in which they demonstrated their unique personality that convinced me to take them on board.

One such choice was Rupert Hampel, a young lawyer who had joined IMG straight after university. He was the perfect example of someone who never disappoints, never lets you down. He was low maintenance, never stressed and always dealt with the next challenge with the same degree of excellence. In no time at all, he became chairman of the board of European Tour Productions, a joint venture between the

European Tour and IMG Media. He was in charge of producing every golf event in Europe four days a week, and selling the live rights to television stations around the world. It was by far the most successful joint venture on our books. I needed someone smart who could manage our most important clients, the All England Lawn Tennis Club (Wimbledon) and Royal and Ancient Golf Club (the R&A). Rupert stepped in with the same smooth level of efficiency. What did I see in Rupert? It's hard to put your finger on it, but he turned out to have the greatest natural ability to manage clients I have ever seen. I could have handed him my biggest account, gone on holiday and slept soundly.

One colleague, Gabrielle, could sell in seven different languages and another, Victor, predicted (correctly) at his interview that we would become best friends. There are many more examples among the people I worked with. Identifying an X-factor is like identifying greatness. You can't necessarily describe it (that, after all, is the reason for the X in X-factor), but you know it when you see it.

What is your X-factor?

The human was not born a predator, but over millions of years of evolution, our brains have turned the instinct of fear into a powerful processor, allowing us to be significantly smarter than our distant predecessors. We calibrate reactions and responses way beyond instinct. We plan, strategize, build, socialize, innovate, anticipate, observe, imagine, fantasize – all of which are different forms of intelligence, independent of our IQ. For example, I have always been fascinated by the way people manage their emotions – those who are persistent in the face of frustration, those who control their temper in the face of distress, the fast learners who excel in the art of observation and experimentation. Each has inherited and developed unique skills that are significant tools in master-crafting their potential.

Some skills are written in your DNA and surface through your life experiences. Some are deep inside of you, and you might not even be aware of them. But never let anyone tell you that you are not capable or dent your self-esteem – you have something that no one else has, and the world would be lesser without you in it. There are a lot of qualities that are not taught at school: understanding people's feelings, empathy, anticipating other people's reactions, controlling stress, creating energy, inspiring trust, charisma, communication, open-mindedness, being popular and not fearing failure.

The list is endless. But you can file them all under X.

CHAPTER 5

THINKING WITH YOUR HEART

Around the year 2000, after a couple of years selling sports programming for IMG, I was made head of sales by my then boss, Bill Sinrich. I had a massive amount of respect for Bill, seeing him as something of a rainmaker; he had used an incredible skill set to build IMG's production arm, TWI, into a global leviathan, taking complex logistical challenges in his stride. As a negotiator, he had a reputation for twisting the corkscrew deeper than anyone else and inventing ways to make multiple margins from the same agreement.

One day he told me, 'Make no mistake, Michel, broadcasters will pay the big bucks because of the quality and exclusivity of the live rights you sell them. Not because they like you personally. So, squeeze the most from every transaction without the fear of being disliked. Your job is to sell the product and get the best price for your client.' The thought of leaving scorched earth behind a ferocious negotiation meant nothing to him. Bill became something of a legend, but I do think that at work he was feared more than loved.

Bill regularly told me off for my managerial approach – I was more than happy to be friendly with everyone I worked with, socializing and having drinks, that kind of thing. Over the months he noticed the close bond I enjoyed with my colleagues, especially in our extra-curricular activities, and gave me an off-record lecture about my management style. But the carrot and stick approach was not in my character and not on my agenda. I understood the need to be firm from time to time, but I couldn't implement a style like his. The team was growing – from 10, to 20, to 50, to 100, to 200, to over 1,000 employees – which in itself required us to adapt some management policies. But I was adamant that I was going to stick to my principles. I wanted to be respected and appreciated, not feared.

Mark McCormack, the original pioneer of IMG and an inspirational leader who I esteemed, died in May 2003, aged 72. In October 2004, Ted Forstmann took over the business, appointing himself chairman and CEO. At that time, Bill

Sinrich was chief executive of TWI. But Bill and Ted's excellent adventure proved to be short lived, with Bill departing after only a little while.

Theodore Joseph Forstmann was a pioneer of debt-funded corporate takeovers, a practice that became known as the leveraged buyout. For many, he was the father of the private equity industry. His fund, Forstmann Little & Company, was involved in buying over 30 different companies, including General Instruments, Dr Pepper and Gulfstream Aerospace Corporation, returning over US$13 billion to his investors.

I took a phone call in London from Ted in spring of 2005, summoning me to a one-to-one dinner at Cipriani, his favourite Italian restaurant in downtown Manhattan. I had been given a day's notice and had no idea what the agenda was. Ted's opening line was, 'Your boss and I have different views so you will take over.' BOOM! I was in a trance for the rest of the dinner.

Afterwards, he invited me to his duplex overlooking Central Park. The concierge welcomed us and when I entered his home I saw paintings by Picasso, Modigliani, Gauguin and Soutine decorating every room.

I had never seen such opulence. But beyond the sheer luxury, there were details telling me this was a special place. Silver-framed black-and-white photos in the living room showed Ted with various US presidents, Ted with Nelson Mandela, Ted with Princess Diana. And so on.

I had to pinch myself. Five hours earlier, I had landed at JFK airport with no idea how the evening would unfold. I asked whether he was sure about his decision concerning Bill. I pointed out that he was very good at what he did and that I was going to have big shoes to fill. 'Yes, indeed,' he responded, 'But nobody is irreplaceable and I want to choose the people I work with, Michel.'

More to life than power

Ted and I got on very well and developed a relationship beyond business: he invited my wife and me on his yacht; we bet on the outcomes of golf games against each other; and we had regular lunches and dinners, animated by entertaining conversations. Unfortunately, our last conversation was a sad occasion; at our last dinner, Ted knew he would not survive an aggressive brain tumour. We spent hours that day talking about philosophy, his legacy, the people he had met and loved, his big breaks and what he was most proud of. I still have goosebumps thinking about it – about the privilege of being invited to share such profound personal insights with a man who knew he was at the end of his days.

I remember that among the silver-framed black-and-white photos hung in his living room, it was not the ones with him and presidents and celebrities that took pride of place. His pride and joy were his sons. As well as a loving adoptive father, he was a major philanthropist, investing in hundreds of millions of dollars in charities, foundations and scholarships to help disadvantaged children get a decent education.

Power and authority don't last forever. The tide rises and falls. If you have been an inspirational mentor or leader, someone who cares for their troops, you will leave a legacy. I have kept in close contact with many of my former colleagues who, for the most part, never turned their back on me when my career took a wrong turn. I still receive calls of affection, wishes of wellbeing and requests for advice, to which I am honoured and delighted to respond.

Bill Sinrich was a skilful negotiator. He taught me a lot, gave me a chance and I owe him. But I do sometimes wonder how someone so sharp did not seem to place that much value on building human relationships with clients.

Acting requires emotional intelligence

Lake Como, in a five-star hotel overlooking one of the most romantic lakes in the world. I had been invited as a guest speaker to participate in the masterclass of the Global General Counsel Forum, one of the most prestigious meetings of the world's top legal and business minds. I was asked to take a dive into the essentials of leadership – the ability to inspire and motivate. I was delighted to have been asked, as it allowed me to speak on something about which I feel very strongly: the question of emotional intelligence versus cognitive intelligence. When it comes to shaping decisions, feelings *matter*.

When we dare to tap into our abilities to observe, analyse, and understand, we are often so much smarter than we think. When we use our curiosity, common sense and wisdom, it allows us to apply some perspective in our behaviour, to stimulate our creativity, inspire and drive opportunities. It allows us to manage from the heart. Such abilities come close to the top of my weaponry. In particular, what I know as social intelligence – interacting with people – is one of my key skills. Regardless of your trade, profession or environment, it is an essential part of everyday life; it was certainly a big part of mine. Strong interpersonal skills will make your journey more productive and more enjoyable. My social appetite helped me to break out of my cocoon at the start, and it quickly became a tool to emancipate myself, contributing in a big way to my personal and professional development.

The process starts with looking into your inner self. Are you *really* interested in people – their capabilities, motivations, moods, feelings and ambitions? Without this interest, you will fail to react to and anticipate the behaviour of others. To be a good mind-reader is a skill, but what you do with such data is even more important. This is what I call emotional interaction. You know instinctively when someone is showing genuine interest in you. If you're not really interested in other people, then deep down you see them as a commodity, something to use. The ability to hear what others cannot, to read body language, detect facial expressions or decode reactions is an asset that will enable you to understand and anticipate the next move of the person in front of you. It allows you to communicate on a profound level as a human being. You will champion effectiveness in organizing groups, managing synergies and building a healthy working environment.

During my career, I enjoyed running motivational workshops and mentoring teams or individuals. I still do this now with passion, giving talks at universities, labs, special societies, conferences and so on. While being prepared is important, spontaneity is the most important vehicle to connect, create impressions and establish new relationships.

Love and respect have always been two critical personal feelings that have driven my relationships. When people like and respect you as an adviser, partner or leader, the reward is so effective that it feels magical. People may *respect* you because you are an operational guru, you have authority, because of your IQ, because you are a rainmaker or because you have leverage over your subordinates. But they will not *love* you for this – social harmony needs the extra human touch.

For over three decades working in a people business, I have been driven by my heart, gut and emotions. My wife would sometimes point out that I seemed more absorbed by my clients and colleagues than my family. It was true that the lifestyle captured me. I was on the road for 200 days a year, the weekdays and weekends merging into one. I was constantly trying to be present in several places at once, desperate not to let anyone down. But the people who surround you see and feel that you have a genuinely caring personality.

There is no academic course that teaches you how to understand people or create relationships. There are no scoring systems that measure how you are perceived by others. But the more attentive you are at reading other people's feelings and understanding their character, the more likely you are to get the best out of them. This, to me, is fundamental – but it is often overlooked. This is applicable in every field, whether politics, arts, management, commerce or personal life.

In my life and work, I have always trusted the emotional ahead of the rational.

CHAPTER 6

NETWORKING WITHOUT LIMITS

In 2010, my family and I moved to a small alpine village in Switzerland, and the first thing that struck us was how polite and respectful the people were. It was part of their general attitude to be good citizens. Absolutely everyone greets each other, in shops and in trains, whether they're out of breath cycling up a hill or just walking in the street. If you don't reciprocate, it's considered rude. You can hear *bonjours* and *au revoirs* from every corner of the street, echoing in a simple but touching harmony. This custom has become second nature to me now, so whenever I venture out of our office in London, or in any other location, I continue to greet and smile at every stranger I come across. Often, the best-case scenario is a blank look. At worst, I get a puzzled expression, with people asking themselves who this weirdo is.

Sharing a smile, exchanging a few kind words or a simple greeting, is not rocket science. Paying compliments, or inquiring about someone, will give you a charm that can win hearts and minds. I like to engage with people about anything and everything. I give compliments and exchange views with a touch of humour. Such conviviality is effortless to me, and the returns are great. Positive body language and an engaging attitude are assets, door-openers, that help start the process of relationship-building – and even if you are not a natural extrovert, the practice of a simple greeting is easy to build! For some, it can feel daunting – but really, interacting deeply with people isn't complicated. Showing genuine interest, searching for common ground or similar passions, engaging in storytelling and inquiring about family wellbeing are just some of the tools at your disposal to help you socialize and progress in building relationships. It leads to likeability, mutual understanding, appreciation, trust and, ultimately, friendship.

It helps me that I tend to assume people are generally good, sincere or well-intentioned. It makes it easier to be natural and friendly if I assume that people are likely to be friendly too! But there is no game plan, roadmap or rulebook. This open attitude and profound sincerity should be spontaneous, and true to you. To some, it comes naturally, but it can be developed to become a part of your X-factor – not everyone will have an interaction style the same as mine. Maybe yours will start with a smile or asking your colleague how their weekend was. For the benefit of your career and your personal life, I encourage you to become a social animal. And start today. Don't wait to count the number of people at your funeral to figure out how popular you are!

When I was around 16, I asked my parents not to come and pick me up every day at school, which was about an hour's drive from home. I wanted to make my own way home because it was a way of meeting people. Sometimes that meant using public transport. Mostly it meant hitchhiking. This is an activity which has almost entirely disappeared – probably with good reason. Because of the risks associated with it, it's illegal in many countries and I certainly would not advocate it as a means of travel now. But for a teenage boy growing up at that time, I never thought of it as dangerous. I saw it as an adventure and never had any problems. Everybody who picked me up was different, from the gregarious to the silent. Some of the people I met were extraordinary. Some left an indelible mark on me and opened my horizons.

One day I was picked up by a young magistrate called Marc. On our drive, he managed to communicate an intense passion about history and the law. This was when I first began to consider studying law after school. We agreed to keep in touch and every year when it was time to prepare for my law exams, I would stay with him and his parents, who ran an open prison at Saint-Hubert, in the Ardennes forest. Over four decades later, we are still friends. And when I can, I always pick up hitchhikers.

The art of relationship-building is something I advocate strongly. This is a key ingredient in maximizing your potential, and it has played a significant role in my journey. Starting from ground zero when I arrived in London, while everyone around me had relatives, friends or contacts in high places, I knew absolutely nobody. I learnt by myself and from scratch. I knew that building a network was essential and there was no time to waste. Starting in the corridors at Nabarro or in the post room at IMG, at the pub, during the weekends, I was fully engaged. It was laborious to begin with, but the process boosted my confidence, presented many opportunities and started to propel my career. Maybe the Brits, and London in particular, provided fertile ground that allowed me to enjoy this exercise. The apparent challenge of being a foreigner and not speaking the language was daunting to start with. But I changed these potential deterrents into an advantage. I was on a mission. This was a 24-hour job in and out of the office, and I became a compulsive socializer.

Working in a sports management company was, of course, the perfect platform to marry work and lifestyle. In no time, I had friends everywhere and developed a reputation as the 'crazy Belgian'. With time, responsibility, seniority and experience, way beyond the contact building, the schmoozing and relationship maintenance, my focus on interacting with people remains very much unchanged and still brings me profound contentment.

Effortless takes effort

As much as socializing was a spontaneous and natural process to me, I tried to put a bit of structure into it, to help me keep track and maximize the benefits. I designed a sheet that I still use today, with three columns. On the left it says 'calls', in the middle it says 'write' and on right it says 'do.' I always have a stack of these to hand, and I monitor my progress by ticking off my tasks, starting a new sheet at the beginning of each week. Originally, I used this as my road map to building networks – but nowadays I use it to serve all purposes. It helps me to keep track of calling so and so, reaching X, Y or Z, organizing to play golf or tennis, attending a party or invites for drinks. It's both work and fun, business and leisure, and it does the job brilliantly.

Maybe you have a more high-tech solution, but the principle is the same – natural, effortless networking and friendships sometimes take organized effort! There is absolutely no shame in using the tools you have at your disposal to help you keep track of your relationships – both for work and for fun.

Network with intention

I used to tell my colleagues to devote time to socializing. To everyone working with me, I would say that time spent outside the office on 'T and E' – travel and entertainment – was a good investment for our division. I don't like having people sitting motionless and glued to a computer – while they might be ticking off their to-do lists, they were neglecting their networks. I would question the senior management team on their social progress: how many new people did you meet this month? Who? What kind of relationship? What has this led you to? We all used to share this information. I tried to lead by example, shooting for the stars and meeting people as highly ranked and as powerful as possible: CEOs, presidents of governing bodies, power brokers, press barons, owners of channels. I wanted us to stimulate each other and push the boundaries.

This, of course, all sounds fairly cynical – after all, we were a sales organization, and there's no denying that the more people you meet, the more people you can potentially do business with. But for me, there was much more to it than that; the spirit of the exercise was, for me, much more profound than simply creating an international database. From contact to acquaintance to business relationship, I wanted my team and me to develop bonds, and in many cases these turned out to become friendships.

Networking on a global scale

During this time, I was all but living on the road, following the sports calendar. On the tennis circuit, I selected the events that became my annual gathering with this community: at the beginning of the year, I would go to the Miami Open, an event owned by IMG and part of the ATP Masters series. I would establish my headquarters at the Ritz Carlton hotel on Key Biscayne. Most of the meetings took place at the Dune Burgers on the Beach bar which turned out to be the office, boardroom and entertainment rendezvous rolled into one.

I would attend two to three tennis Majors per year, starting with Roland Garros in Paris for three to four days, followed by Wimbledon. For Wimbledon, we rented a house shared between the media guys and the tennis division – this was the most exhausting fortnight of the calendar. We had meetings all day, starting with breakfast followed by lunch, client entertainment at the marquee situated in the club grounds, Pimms, parties, reunions of all sorts, and ended the day with dinners and after-dinners. The whole worldwide business community was in town. It was both amazing and an absolute killer.

The US Open in New York was no less intense. I had my routines, which most often ended up with me joining Gavin Forbes, the larger-than-life South African head of IMG's tennis division, in his den at the Snafu Bar on 127 East 47th Street. Everyone gathered here at some stage during the night, including coaches, agents, broadcasters and officials from governing bodies. This was the fishing pond at which you could hook new relationships.

Aside from tennis, I replicated the exercise with the golf circuit. The British Open and the Ryder Cup were a must, along with the PGA at Wentworth. I was a regular guest of my close clients and friends at Rolex, for whom IMG Media produced tailor-made programming to activate their high-end communication campaign in the sport. I had the privilege of being invited to play in pro-am events around the world with the most talented golfers, and was introduced to prestigious decision-makers at these events. This glamorous VIP lifestyle was my fairway to heaven!

Aside from golf and tennis, there were so many exciting events on the calendar. The Moto GP in Barcelona was a high-octane experience, although once I thought it might be literally the end of the road for me when the hyperactive Manel Arroyo, managing director of Dorna, which owned MotoGP, took me on a ride around the track! The finals of the Rugby World Cup in France, London and Japan, and the Opening Ceremonies of the

Olympics in Beijing, Vancouver and London, were also memorable adventures where I discovered so many extraordinary personalities in so many incredible settings. I felt privileged to be there – and to be paid for it – but I also knew that I had earned my passage to these great theatres of life, sport and entertainment. This was my job.

This is all to say that this complete whirlwind of globe-trotting and socializing was more than a full-time job. My briefcase was my office (I still own the same one that accompanied me from day one). My hotel room became my home, and a phone was my lifeline. I don't want to show my age, but at the start it was about finding a public telephone box and having coins of the local currency – a far cry from Zoom calls! At the peak of my career, IMG Media was managing an average of eight events a day somewhere in the world. The European Tour for four days a week, the ATP tour, a vast number of football leagues, motor racing, volleyball, snooker, rugby, sailing, badminton. This list goes on. We had over 200 clients aggregating over 40,000 hours of live programming. I had the choice of being at eight different places any day of the year, and that was just to meet our clients before the day job started. This was a monster to manage from an operational and relationship perspective, but together with a team of highly skilled individuals with a fantastic collaborative spirit, not only did we manage but we delivered at a high level of excellence.

Among the many incredible trips I have been on, one that always comes to mind happened in 2003. Alinghi, the sailing team of biotech billionaire Ernesto Bertarelli, was competing in the Louis Vuitton Cup in New Zealand, and IMG had been retained to produce and distribute the live pictures of the challenger series and the Americas Cup. My former colleague Michel Hodara, who was in charge of the media and subsequently became the CEO of the prestigious event, offered to put me up at his home in Auckland. I flew in from London and spent the day with the production crew on fast boats and helicopters following the teams. In the evening, I was entertained at the harbour, which had been transformed into a giant party venue, until late in the evening – so late, in fact, that I didn't have time to make use of Michel's hospitality. I was already on my way to Melbourne for the Australian Open, where I assisted Paul McNamee, the CEO of the Open, with the renewal of his Eurosport contract. From there it was a hop to our office in Hong Kong for further meetings before eventually returning home.

At IMG, that was a 'week in the office'.

Networking can take you anywhere

IMG is synonymous with sport, but I was keen to branch out and develop a business in the entertainment field. This too is a people business, dependent on building human relationships. I started with music concerts first, signing a distribution deal for the concert in memory of the late Princess Diana at Althorp Park on 27 June 1998. A couple of years later, I signed with women's underwear brand Victoria's Secret for the media distribution of its fashion show, which was held in Cannes in May 2000, in synch with the famous film festival. The show was sold to many non-sports channels too, but was also available live on the internet. The World Wide

Web was in its infancy in those days, and the broadband infrastructure couldn't handle large numbers of contemporaneous live streams. When the Victoria's Secret models hit the catwalk, the internet melted. The models, many of whom were managed by IMG, had arrived by Concorde, painted pink for the occasion. After the show, my friend and colleague Michael Mellor and I were invited for the gala cocktail dinner. We tried to make the most of the occasion, exchanging professional tips and handing out business cards. Can you imagine handing a business card to the likes of Liz Taylor, Gregory Peck, Elton John, James Caan, Elizabeth Hurley and Sean Penn? It was a 'who's who' of celebrities from the worlds of fashion, Hollywood and music, mixing with models like Laetitia Casta and Heidi Klum. Everything was over the top. Despite our best efforts, while we tried to engage in conversations, I do not recall making any contacts. Still, it was fun trying!

Things didn't always go as expected, but there was always an opportunity to make new contacts. In 2003, I convinced Julia Morley, former model and chairman and CEO of the Miss World

Organization, that we would generate more revenue and exposure for her contest than her distribution set-up at the time. This was another wild bet, venturing into the unknown, but we instantly got on very well. The next Miss World was held at the Sanya beach resort in Hainan province, in the far south of China. It was the first time the country had hosted the event. My people had done a very decent job generating record visibility worldwide, agreeing exclusive broadcasting rights deals with hundreds of channels. I arrived in the morning expecting to have a relaxing day and to show my commitment towards Julia, my client. It was far from relaxing. In order to promote this tropical island as the new tourist destination, the local government had granted free access to media companies left, right and centre, driving a coach and horses through the finely crafted exclusivity clauses in the contracts with our broadcast partners.

The crown was placed on the head of Rosanna Davison, the daughter of the singer Chris de Burgh, and I had the pleasure of socializing with Chris that evening. I flew back early the next morning following the after-party, once again not having used my hotel room. Back in the office, I was asked how things were and I said, 'I went to China yesterday. It was a disaster. I managed to have a few pleasant encounters though.' The point is this: inertia was not an option. Socializing was a never-ending activity at the heart of my profession, and if relationships could be made or sustained, then nothing was ever a complete bust.

Dos and don'ts

After a while, I started to establish guidelines that governed the way I developed relationships across the globe. It is important to stay in contact with people you meet along the way, and show support and compassion if they have a downturn in their career. That's partly, of course, because it's just the right thing to do – human beings need compassion – but when they bounce back, as almost everyone will at some point, your relationship will be stronger than ever. In the same spirit, the key to relationship-building is to establish and maintain a rapport *beyond the point of expectation*. By this I mean that you aim to have a relationship because you want to, rather than because you need to. With no other purpose, I keep in touch, make occasional calls, show attention, send personalized Christmas cards, inquire about the family, provide support and give advice. Do not reach out to people only when you need them. If anything, this can be counterproductive.

Reach for the stars

Dis-moi qui tu fréquentes et je te dirai qui tu es is a popular French proverb, which translates as, 'Tell me who you hang out with and I'll tell you who you are'. This is true, but I would invite everyone to take it as an invitation and opportunity – not as a cautionary tale. I have reached out to top guns in my time, and even if there was some apprehension occasionally, the exercise can be rewarding. Often, reaching out to people who could be perceived as 'out of my league' turned out to lead to interactions that were surprisingly pleasant, fruitful and fun. Finding the groove or a hook to engage with rich, famous or powerful individuals may seem challenging, and indeed they may well have limited windows for you, but remember they are as human as you and I. Don't be scared.

One such occasion was when I met Johann Rupert, the multi-billionaire South African chairman of the Richemont luxury goods group, parent company to brands like Cartier, Dunhill, Van Cleef & Arpels and Montblanc. He's been lionized as businessman, entrepreneur and leader of the year by more countries and international organizations than there is space for here. Men like Rupert have an aura, and it's easy to assume they are inaccessible, but if you don't try, you'll never find out. I spotted Johann alone on the terrace of the VIP village of the exclusive Royal Zoute Golf Club at Knokke-Heist in Belgium, which was hosting the Belgian Open. Dunhill was sponsoring the event. I introduced myself and we had a few drinks together. It was a most extraordinary exchange. He was nonchalant but captivating. I originally felt under pressure about what I could say to sustain the attention of someone so powerful, but not only did we have a fun exchange, we actually stayed in touch.

He is one of the most passionate and accessible individuals I have ever met.

Rupert regularly attends major events in golf and he closely follows the South African rugby team. At each of these events, I tried to reach out to him, usually with a good degree of success. I saw him at St Andrews hitting balls on the practice ground during the Open again. I approached him to say hi and to congratulate him on the quality of his swing. I asked him who was going to win the Open that week and he told me to put my money on John Daly. On the final Sunday, I was in his suite at the Old Course Hotel following live with one eye on the TV and one on the course over the balcony. On that 23 July 1995, after a four-hole play-off against Constantino Rocca, John Daly lifted the trophy! It was an honour to be in his entourage. If I had not 'crossed the road' and introduced myself at Royal Zoute, this would not have happened.

I had this fantasy of participating in the Olympics once. With my old friend Hubert, my future brother-in-law Paul, and my brother Phillipe, we decided to create – from nothing – the Belgian bobsleigh team. Without any fear, and very much along the lines of the Jamaican bobsleigh team of *Cool Runnings* fame, we entered our first event in Winterberg in Germany at the European Championships in November 1989. One of our rival competitors was Prince Albert of Monaco. I reached out to him, and we struck up a rapport that deepened from one race to another. Things came to an abrupt end when I crashed the bobsleigh badly, nearly killing my brother. But since then, I have often run into Prince Albert, either at the Sportel trade fair in Monaco, or at the Olympic Games. The point is, sometimes you end up building high-level relationships without realizing it at the time, simply by investing time in the right people. That junior that some executives may overlook could one day be the boss.

When I moved to Paris, I got in contact with one of my Belgian clients, Geert Broos, who had moved to Procter and Gamble in Paris at the same time. I offered to share a small house in Puteaux, near La Défense business district. A few years later, I was in Bombay for the cricket and was at the breakfast buffet when someone tapped me on my shoulder. 'Geert, what are you doing here?' I asked. He had become head of Coca-Cola India. People grow in parallel with your career, and many will do better than you. Another example concerns an ambitious Belgian doctor who was head of the orthopaedic department at the Ghent hospital. This doctor was a former Olympic sailor, who participated in three Olympics, and a sports medicine lecturer. At the time I was running the IMG office in Brussels, another 'famous' Belgian, Eric Drossart, who started the IMG media business in Europe, took me under his wing and introduced me to this doctor. Eric advised me to follow him, as he was going to try and become the next president of the Belgian Olympic Committee. His name was Jacques Rogge. I followed Eric's orders, and indeed Jacques not only became the head of the Belgian Olympic Committee, but the president of the International Olympic Committee, the ultimate role in sport. Among other things, Rogge initiated the Youth Olympic Games. In 2020, my son Louis, who's a keen skier, was flag carrier for Belgium at the 2020 Youth Olympic Games in Lausanne. You never know where relationships will lead.

Networking is what I have done all my life and still do today – perhaps with less intensity now, but with the same passion and pleasure. I love people and people seem to like me. This is how simply I can describe the equation. I socialized everywhere, all the time, with many types of people: businesspeople, celebrities, intellectuals, financiers, athletes and sometimes just fun people with big hearts. It has taken up a big part of my time and energy, often to the detriment of my family life.

My daughter Charlotte was once asked at school what her father did for a living. She replied that her dad's job was to go around the world visiting nightclubs and restaurants. Looking back, it really hits me when I look at the family photo albums my wife Sarah kept meticulously. I reflect on the value of time. All these experiences make up the narrative of my life. I think about whether it's possible to balance professional ambition – going that extra mile to over-achieve, with all the benefits that entails – with the high cost of being away from home, far from one's family, with all the sacrifices that entails.

Networking without limits was only possible because Sarah did such an amazing job of raising our three well-balanced kids and because she did so with such passion. We were a good team, and I would never have put myself in the role of the man insisting the woman stays at home if I had sensed any member of the team was not completely comfortable in their role. I am sure I did not take her for granted.

I do now have a sense of guilt, however, for prioritizing my passion over other things. I am catching up now, but I feel sorry for not having spent more time at home, for which I apologize to my whole family. I have advocated throughout the book that you should have fun and enjoy life, not just chase success. I guess I have suggested you can have your cake and eat it. But it involves making choices, and those choices have consequences. In all honesty, I believe I would make the same choices again regarding my life and career, but only because I know that in our case the teamwork was so strong and genuine.

I turned my passion into a business, and this became my life: networking without limits.

CHAPTER 7

THE EXPERT WAS ONCE A BEGINNER

The next few pages are for me to share some tips that have aided me in my personal journey. As I have said, your grades and your CV are no guarantee of success. And even if they help open the door for you, the leap from theory to practice is one you will have to make by yourself, without a safety net and without the helping hand of parents or teachers. You will gain wisdom and build your confidence through a succession of experiments, through trial and error, on your journey.

Hopefully, some of these tips will inspire you in the quest to create your own future.

Experiment as early as possible

Before undertaking her degree at the University of Edinburgh, my eldest daughter, Charlotte, had held six different summer jobs requiring three different languages – French, Spanish and English. The tasks she was given ranged from making the morning coffee to translating interviews, or simply being a runner from one desk to another. She started at the bottom and began to demystify the unknown world of work.

While taking her degree, and after graduation, she secured several internships. These ranged from an Erasmus scholarship working for EuroLeague basketball in Barcelona to working in online education in London, working in data management in Melbourne, being a marketing assistant in Hong Kong and acting as a media rights assistant at UEFA in Nyon, Switzerland. It has become increasingly common for young people to take a gap year, either before or after graduation. That can be great fun, and a great opportunity to learn and grow. Charlotte decided to sacrifice the fun, however, to dive straight into the corporate world – to learn the trade from the inside. After a couple of years, she decided to deepen her understanding of the business by enrolling for a Master's degree at the ESADE business school in Barcelona. The choices that now lie ahead of her include going back into the corporate world or flying with her own wings and starting a business. Whatever path she chooses, she has embraced experimentation to build up a unique profile for herself, with experience based on tasting the real thing at an early stage and building communities of real friends.

I am an advocate of internships. At IMG, I used such opportunities to test the practical ability, motivation and ambition of people who would later be given proper challenges and responsibilities. Many of the talents that came through the IMG internship programme went to the very top, driven by hard work and determination, as well as their innate abilities. This was how my own journey started too. I wanted to get my foot in the door and internship was a way. I was determined to break any barrier to have the privilege of jumping on the corporate ladder, building relationships and learning the trade. However you are able to get your start, I recommend that you get on the dance floor as soon as the party starts and show off your moves, regardless of how outrageous or clumsy they might be. Practice, goodwill, hard work and experimentation are prerequisites for the journey to success.

You may be a talented artist, a gifted athlete or possess a scientific intellect, but without experimentation and practice, you are not yet a star. You may like cooking and feel passionate about it, but to become a recognized chef you will need to go beyond reading recipes. It is about hard work, experimenting, innovating, taking inspiration from others, creating and progressing. No one starts as an expert. You may be gifted, talented and well educated, but the path to knowledge is practice and the earlier you take a deep dive the better: to experiment, to learn languages, to see the world, to taste real things. It is never too early to start. Do not waste time; the journey is shorter than you think.

Observe aggressively

My grandfather was a street-smart guy and made a few bucks on the way, but he was quick to disabuse us of the idea that the fruit of his labours would pave the way for an easy life for his descendants. On the other hand, he was most generous when it came to what I call 'family experiences' – what other people call holidays. From the age of 11, he took his tribe – 15 of us, the grandparents, their children and their respective families – on adventurous Christmas breaks. I saw the world from very different angles.

Whether intentional or not, he gave us all the travel bug. He made me curious to see how the world works. I became fascinated by foreign culture, and whenever possible I picked up my backpack and off I went. I would have little or no money in my pocket, but I enjoyed surviving on my wits – hitchhiking, sleeping rough, staying with people along the way. By the age of 20, I had travelled the five continents. I was passionate about different civilizations, climates, cuisines and peoples' attitudes. Observing was a form of entertainment.

In 1985, I got a call from Clive, a Zimbabwean acquaintance who offered me a chance at the last minute to join a small group going down the Zambezi River. It was brutally hard. For a week we lived in our canoes with the bare necessities. We paddled between the crocs and the hippos.

We slept on the sandbank with only a mosquito net between us and the wild animals. I learned that I was a tolerated element in nature. I realized I had not been using senses like smell, sight, hearing – all primary components of survival in such an environment. That trip changed my understanding of what observation means.

When it was my turn to raise a family, I put observation at the centre of the education process. Once a year, the five of us embarked on an adventurous trip. We took a trip to Rwanda to help with some of the Right to Play charitable initiatives. We gave classes and played football with local children. Right to Play is an international non-profit organization that helps children to overcome the effects of war, poverty and disease through play.

While we were there, we trekked for hours to reach a family of gorillas to spend a magical moment with them in their natural habitat. We were accepted by these imposing silverbacks, our distant cousins. On another occasion, we devoted the afternoon to following a mother cheetah teaching her cubs how to hunt, and on yet another we spent the night in the cold listening to lions hunting buffalo.

Observing nature fascinated us all; it was more of a life experience than anything else. It was never about chilling on a beach somewhere and doing nothing all day; instead, it was about observation and discovery. In August 2016, my wife and I took our daughters camping in the Okavango Delta in Botswana, one of the most beautiful places on earth if you love the wilderness as we do. We missed some early warning signs made by a herd of elephants and had to gallop away through the bushes to save our lives. In some environments, observing is more than a simple form of entertainment. It's a means of survival.

In 1991, I had been in the IMG job for a few years, but I was overtaken by a need to search and reinvent myself. I was not sure why or where to go, but I had this burning desire to drop everything and see the world. I went to see my boss, Ian Todd, to break the news. The conversation was short. 'How long for?' he asked. 'I don't know – perhaps a year,' I responded. He answered, 'If you are back in six months, I'll wait for you. If not, good luck. I envy you.' That was it. I headed east and came back six months later from the west. In St Petersburg I jumped the Trans-Siberian railway to Beijing, cycled down through China, climbed to the base camp of the Annapurna massif in the Himalayas and sailed in the South Pacific. I applied this same attitude of curiosity in my professional environment, and this passion for observation has probably enhanced my social intelligence. When you can look beyond prejudice, established beliefs, stereotypes and social stigma, what you discover is valuable in helping you to understand other people's perspectives. Are you dealing with a patient, composed and relaxed individual, or are you facing a strong-minded, erratic control freak? I cannot imagine how you can go anywhere without trying to comprehend who you are dealing with or understand how others perceive you. This does not need to be some profound analytical exercise – it's about feeling. I need to have these cards in my deck before I play. Observe who you are selling to, observe who you are working for, observe who you are operating with, observe who you can negotiate a compromise with. As I learned on my adventurous trips, don't take what you see for granted. These are clues to read, analyse, process. This data will help you understand, anticipate and imagine. Having identified the forces present, and knowing their potential behavioural impact, you can write your game plan and design your strategy. Make the wrong assessment and you increase your chances of failure.

Observe the cast of the play

In 2015, we had an embryonic division at IMG based on sports betting. It was run by Freddie Longe, one of our most clever and innovative young executives. We had started to feel the heat from competitors who were more established players in the market, so we had to react, to make substantial investments, to adopt an aggressive strategy and take a few risks. I knew that Freddie had the potential to take on such a challenge, but he was daunted, given his limited experience of decision-making at this level. It seemed like David versus Goliath to him. I could see that Freddie's creative talents were held in check by the scale of the challenge. He was concerned about engaging company funds and taking a risk with money that wasn't his. It was the ultimate honest reaction. We established an unwritten rule between us: if something was a success, he would take the credit; and if it was a failure, it would be down to me. After that, he never let me down and has always over-delivered. It was through observation and understanding of his character that we were able to create a progressive relationship. The gaming division subsequently enjoyed the most dramatic growth in our history, largely thanks to Freddie and his team.

Observe anything and everything. Look at how things are made, scrutinize how dysfunctional certain organizations are, look at historical data, appreciate the way the world has evolved. All these things will sharpen your instinct, boost your ability to act and react, stimulate your anticipation, and build your confidence. In your day-to-day life, feel every sound, every smell, every movement, and your brain will naturally become accustomed to analysing and processing such data. This exercise will prepare you, consciously or unconsciously, to anticipate and be a better decision-maker. Observe with a passion.

Observation leads to creativity and imagination, and imagination can lead anywhere.

Engage in a charm offensive

Whether we like it or not, people judge a book by its cover. From the starting block, you need to create an impression. You may be a natural charmer or you may play the long game, but my advice is that from the word go you need to impress – by the way you look, laugh, behave, shake hands, pronounce your first word or smile, you will send signals that will affect how you are perceived by people around you. Whether it's exuding a sense of trustworthiness or triggering a feeling of dislike, be aware that from the get-go you have entered the ring.

I remember the first time I was introduced to Mark McCormack, two to three years into the job. In the London summer at first light, around 6.00 am, I used to drive to Wentworth Golf Club. Arriving before the staff and the gardeners, I would just wander in and tee off, regularly managing to squeeze 10 to 12 holes before heading to the office. I could not afford the membership, but I thought that nobody would notice or question my audacity. I was never caught and my early-morning habits got me a bit of a reputation in the office. When I shook Mark's hand for the first time, he said, 'Oh, you are the guy who plays golf before everyone arrives at the office.' That was his first impression of me, for better or worse!

People are constantly making snap judgements, good or bad. It is not much of an effort to send positive vibrations through a warm handshake, a welcoming smile and genuine words of interest. Interpersonal skills built on likeability are increasingly important in a society fuelled by 'likes'. Can you learn to be charming? I believe it originates in spontaneous charisma, and it may be more difficult for some, but yes, you can condition your brain to send positive vibrations. Once you have changed your mindset, the rest will follow. The people around you will feel your vibes even before you open your mouth. Look in your locker for weapons of seduction. Show interest, listen, read people, observe, find common ground, compliment, use humour and self-deprecation – the list is endless. Charming people is a skill. Never underestimate the power of being the nice guy; even in the context of disagreement, keep your charming armour on. I am a winner (mostly!) and have the blood of a sore loser. The industry I was involved in was very much about winning accounts and doing a better job than the competition. With IMG being the market leader, everyone was against us, and I constantly felt under attack. I learnt to be smart in defeat. I started congratulating my opponents when losing business or offered them a hand of collaboration moving forward. This was part of my charm offensive. The wind will turn, and the situation will come back in your favour faster by adopting such an attitude.

Another state of mind that I find very effective in building trust is the 'give attitude'. It makes me genuinely happy to be generous, whether in my time for others, giving advice with no expected return, small gifts or attention, compassion, compliments, just saying some nice words to provide a bit of affection. This is not an effort; it's a spontaneous attitude. There is no hard work in this. Planting good seeds will bring you an abundant harvest. I like to call people regularly, often for no specific reason, just to say, 'Hi, how are you?' I send Christmas messages to thank people for their hard work and their friendship, not because it's an obligation but because I like to reach out and show my appreciation. I start or finish conversations by inquiring about people's health and family. How is the spouse doing? How are the kids? Saying thank you for someone's time, invitation or good advice is important, and is not mere politeness – it's vital in making people feel valued.

I have spent many days throughout my career entertaining customers worldwide, clients and friends. Breakfasts, lunches and dinners were an integral part of the exercise, but I also wanted to bring an extra touch and make a difference to how we were interacting with our client base. I wanted to generate positive impressions, putting quality before quantity, and highlighting how creative and effective our organization could be perceived as being. With over 200 sales executives across five continents, an average of eight events a day, 200 clients that we represented and close to 1,000 customers, we were in a constant mood of social business interaction.

Take these three illustrations:

Sportel

Every October, the whole sports and media circus congregates in Monaco for the Sportel convention, under the patronage of HSH Prince Albert II. Decision-makers, promoters, agencies, broadcasters, the trade press, federations, leagues, producers, tech and software providers, betting companies and digital gurus of all sorts mingle in the principality. This amounts to 4,000 attendees, 1,000 companies and exhibitors from 70 countries engaging in a three-day business speed-dating event at the Grimaldi Forum.

IMG had a presence, but I thought that trying to be first among equals with a stand selling our products was the wrong message for us to send. At the time, we had over 40 offices around the world and, unlike smaller operators, we did not need to be at Sportel to get noticed, so we took a different path from the others. I rented the prestigious terrace of the Hotel de Paris, overlooking the Ligurian sea, and threw a classy cocktail party to which we invited our community. In a short time, this rendezvous became the place to see and be seen. It set the right relaxed tone, but also sent a subliminal message: we are the market leaders, and we do things differently.

Cowboys up!

One event I always looked forward to was the pro bull-riding finals in Las Vegas. Around 2005, I had the pleasure of meeting Randy Bernard, the CEO of Professional Bull Riders, Inc. in my London office. It would be difficult to find someone friendlier and more open and enthusiastic than Randy. The late Barry Frank, the New York media guru and IMG/TWI executive vice president, suggested Randy reach out to me, as he was looking to partner with an international agent who would promote his sport on the world stage.

Randy was very committed and I was sorry to tell him that this project would be difficult to take on with any chance of success. It was due to be a very short meeting, but he talked passionately about the bull-breeding industry and the fitness and daredevil attitude of the riders, whose goal was to last seven seconds on the back of a raging monster. Randy also explained that the sport was enjoying tremendous growth. The association started with a handful of riders each throwing US$1,000 into the kitty and recently he had turned down a US$50 million takeover bid. I told Randy what he had asked me was as challenging as getting *pétanque* live on ESPN, but said that if he would consider a 'promotional budget' to market his product, rather than us taking a commission to try to sell it, I would consider it. Randy and I shook hands on the US$50,000 deal to promote the Las Vegas final event.

I got on the phone straight away with my team of hardcore European sales executives, explained the situation and set them the mission of giving away (not selling) the two-hour show. Whoever was successful in securing some form of broadcast coverage would be invited with his broadcaster client for a 'get-to-know-better' experience in Las Vegas to learn about the sport. Whatever happens in Vegas stays in Vegas, of course... but it was special to say the least! Randy's hosting magic made people feel like VIPs, and we became best friends. For the closing dinner,

Randy invited everyone, including bull riders and bull breeders, to one of the best restaurants in town and we learnt the 'cowboys up' tradition. It involves downing a shot of Jack Daniels. Very simple. But we practised a lot.

To end on a high, I told Randy that if he was prepared to double his promotional budget, we would secure a worldwide TV audience bigger than his US coverage. Deal. All our European broadcast partners became excited about the sport, taking on the series as well as the final. And we also did deals with broadcasters in China, Brazil, Australia and Argentina. We easily surpassed our target. The next year in Vegas, we were welcomed like true celebrities, with the police escorting us to and from the arena. The closing dinner was another triumphant celebration, punctuated with many 'cowboys up'. Together, we had created the dynamics of the 'fastest growing sport in the world'. Interest was created through this promotional kick-start, but in subsequent years broadcasters started paying proper licence fees for the rights, to reflect rising audience ratings. On 15 April 2015, Endeavor (formerly WME/IMG) acquired the company.

'Cowboys up' became the rallying cry to kick-start every international IMG sales conference!

The grappa experience

In 2010, Ioris Francini signed a distribution agreement with RCS Sport, a sports and media company that owns one of the biggest road cycling events, the Giro d'Italia. During one of our gatherings in Singapore, we brainstormed ideas to promote the event on the world stage. Late one night, we had the idea of a pro-am (professional and amateur) version of the Giro, something common in golf but almost unheard of then in cycling. We invited a number of existing and future broadcasters to live the Giro experience on the bike, discovering in person the same beautiful back roads used by the pros.

When the dynamic Paolo Bellino became director general of RCS Sport in 2014, we used the tradition to take relationship-building to a deeper level. Nearly a decade later, a close group of a dozen friends meet once a year for this unique occasion. The guest list includes event owners, brand managers, bankers, media power brokers and senior people from governing bodies. We are all motivated by a desire to stretch ourselves to our mental and physical limits in a true spirit of camaraderie. We have cycled through the most picturesque roads together – on the Costa Smeralda in Sardinia, hugging the Amalfi Coast south of Naples – and we have climbed the volcanic Mount Etna in Sicily in all sorts of weather conditions. We reward ourselves with the best food and wine that this country can offer. Every time we see each other, individually or collectively, we have a grappa to celebrate our friendship.

A charm offensive is a great concept and a way to start relationships. But ultimately, people will love and respect you for your genuine commitment.

Stage fright

Life is an accumulation of experiences. No one is born with knowledge, and of course no one will ever be perfect in their journey to success. Some try harder than others and learn fast from error and failure. Others get freaked out by their mistakes, and only progress at a snail's pace. Or worse, they give up. We all have wings, and we all can fly – like the little bird on the edge of the nest. How early we fly, and how high we can go, is the challenge.

Every achiever is inhibited by a degree of fear or apprehension. The actor or public speaker who walks on stage, the politician who picks up the mic, the boxer who bounces around in the corner of the ring, the golfer who practises their swing on the first tee, the racing pilot on the grid, the skier at the starting gate – all are confronted with a feeling of fear, whether they're an amateur or an experienced pro. Fear is *natural*. It is a biological thing, ingrained within the human being. If you're not afraid to fail, it probably means you don't care enough; and if you're not prepared to go for the kill, it's unlikely that you will succeed. Fear gives you energy. The degree of uncertainty in early challenges may be daunting – perhaps you are consumed by an inferiority complex or intimidated by dominant characters. But if frozen by doubt, you will not transcend yourself and will have to look on while others seize their chance.

The more you try, prepare and practise, the more you will build up confidence. With failure, you will understand what to change and how to improve in order to improve your chances the next time around.

As Michael Jordan put it, 'I have failed over and over again in my life. And that is why I succeed.' Tennis legend Martina Navratilova said, 'Once you start believing in yourself, anything is possible. Once you start believing in yourself, your dreams take place. The more you believe, the more you achieve.'

I was scared of venturing into the unknown just like anyone else – scared of making mistakes, scared of ridicule. I was apprehensive before my first sales presentation, and my first attempt at public speaking. I was this young expat with broken English placing myself in the arena with powerful international businessmen. Yet I was committed to making this journey as adventurous, fun and enriching as possible. At this early point in my career, I did not have much to lose. I took all the negative thoughts out of the equation: there was nothing life threatening in giving it my best shot. What was the worst that could have happened to me? Going back to where I started? Big deal. While in this frame of mind, I wanted to occupy the space as much as possible. Naïve but with a big heart, I was prepared to take hits and make the best of the opportunities presented. This was me. This was my passion, and I believed I had a chance. I was craving advice, to be directed or mentored. I was reaching out for any help I could get, of course, but in the end it was me and the elements. I was drawing my energy from my own guts. It was not an easy ride. I faced uncertainty and doubts. I blundered, made a fool of myself, said the wrong things at the wrong times to the wrong people. I have cringed often, but I managed to swallow these frustrations and turn them into fuel for improvement.

If you, as a young entrepreneur, have fought with bankruptcy, or as a child have suffered parental loss, or been discriminated against for racial, educational or gender reasons, it can make you hungry for revenge and to become a bigger achiever. This is the type of paradox that can catapult an individual to success against all the odds. There is a form of mental alchemy, ignited by fears, setbacks or handicaps, that will drive you further and higher than your peers who have had an easy upbringing. Reveal your potential with audacity.

To all the budding Eddie the Eagles out there: have a dream, do not be deterred by failure. Your determination will bring achievements.

No guts, no glory!

The art of anticipation

A dependence on conventional wisdom will drown your individualism and make you one of the crowd. On the other hand, a progressive life and an ambitious soul will prepare you better for rapidly evolving circumstances. Getting off the beaten track and embracing the unknown requires skills, such as the ability to anticipate and innovate. To morph into an innovator, you will need the ability and willingness to design solutions to unpredicted problems. To create the business model of tomorrow will require a 'rainmaking' dimension to your personality.

During my 30 years in sports management, what I enjoyed the most was that there were rarely two days the same. I was always looking at ways to stimulate the pioneering spirit of our enterprise, to rebel against conformity and drive innovation, both individually and collectively. The culture was about creating a new dimension that would make our business unique, captivating, profitable and rich in opportunities. I was not about to follow the rules of those who had gone before. I was more excited about disrupting the status quo and taking on the establishment. I regularly gathered groups of executives with the same attitude, and under the banner of 'business development meetings' we morphed into a sect of mercenaries planning their next battle – anticipating the business model of tomorrow. Returning money to investors, pleasing the directors, boosting financial projections, increasing the profit margin, gaining bonuses, accolades and positions of respect. All this was the name of the game for me. I got the biggest kick from new business and creative thinking. I got my adrenaline more from the innovative side of the business.

I have always been inspired by McCormack's vision of the future and how he saw the evolution of the business he invented. He started by representing the commercial interests of the *crème de la crème* in every sport. From sports celebrities, Mark expanded into representing opera singers and models, and even did business with the Pope. His calling card was staying ahead to avoid being copied by the competition. He moved into the business of events management and represented what are still today some of the biggest governing bodies in the sports industry: the International Olympic Committee, Wimbledon, The Open Championship and the Rugby World Cup, to name a few. When sports became a mega media business, the growth of IMG was exponential. The evolution of technology and the new ways to monetize rights strengthened our position as market leaders. Mark regularly gathered his teams, senior management and special task forces to lead us through his futuristic view of the business. At the end of the dinner, he used to pull his small handwritten cards – impossible for anyone else to read – from his inside pocket and drip-feed us messages, illustrations, strategic directions, reflections and examples of what to do and what not to do. When I had the honour of being invited to one of these evenings, I attended as though I was a tolerated apostle at the Last Supper.

One night we were at the Bay Hill Club & Lodge, the golf club home of Arnold Palmer in Florida. Mark wanted to pick the brains of a dozen media executives. He took us through a long list, but to be honest there was no electricity in the air. This was not an enthusiastic exchange to say the least. Undeterred, he came up with two more concepts. The first was the idea of bringing ballroom dancing into the sports arena and, in the context of a very lucrative skating business, mixing sport and entertainment. As if this idea was not enough to send us to sleep, he then suggested a cooking competition where all participants would be given the same ingredients and recipe with expert chefs judging the outcome. We looked at each other. Us, the sports buff, adrenaline junkies. We exchanged embarrassed looks, wondering whether the old man had started to lose his touch. Mark had imagined, 20 years before their time, two of the most successful television franchises ever: *Strictly Come Dancing* and the *Bake Off*. But we turned him down! His spirit of innovation and his art of anticipation were without equal, and those qualities drove the business many years after he had left us. He still inspires me to this day.

IMG Media was by far the leading independent production and distribution company in sports. However, innovation was its essence. We were anticipating that technology would transform the business of broadcasting, impacting the way in which rights would be carved out, segmented and monetized in the future. We created a series of new sources of revenue, ranging from audio, closed circuit, video-on-demand (VOD), betting data, over-the-top (OTT) and news clips. In one of our business development sessions, a couple of inspired young innovators, including Richard Wise, anticipated that technology would one day enable live broadcast of sports on planes and on ships at sea. We set about acquiring the exclusive broadcasting rights for the most popular events, including the Olympics, the Premier League, the UEFA Champions League, the FIFA World Cup, the UEFA European Championship and the Majors of golf and tennis for closed-circuit exploitation on channels that did not yet exist. Sport24 was born. There was literally nowhere on earth where you could find a sports channel that good. It could only be seen at sea or in the skies.

Once the technology had been developed, IMG started charging airlines and cruise ship companies per plane and per ship on a monthly basis. A few years later, the numbers were incredible. I still praise Richard Wise and his team for their role in this masterpiece of anticipation, for seeing ahead of anyone else a way to capture the attention of passengers in international waters and in the skies.

With the art of anticipation, the sky is literally the limit for the rebel transformers of tomorrow.

CHAPTER 8

THE SEARCH FOR MEANING

When I was 16, I wanted to be a sports hero; in my twenties, I hoped to be a rock star; and in my thirties, I simply wanted to embrace professional success. Over the following two decades, though, I started to develop the desire to balance success with contentment. Beyond your quest for success, what drives you?

Da Vinci's Vitruvian Man embodies a vision where art and science collide, stimulating the mind to probe timeless questions about who we are and how we fit in – the role that we want to play in the grand order of the universe. I had the picture above my bed at university and would study it. At the intersection of the earthly and the cosmic, what does our brief spark of life amount to? What do we want to do with such a precious instant? The search for meaning is not something you can put off until you retire and have time on your hands.

Asking the big questions

Like most of us, from an early age I have asked the fundamental questions about life. What comes after death? Who is God? What is my mission on the planet? What is the meaning of life? What is the purpose of existence? Raised as a Catholic, I initially had all these questions answered for me by someone else. At boarding school, I was praying first thing in the morning, before lunch and dinner, attending evening Mass and confessing sins that I didn't know I was committing. The definition of good and bad was neither a dialogue nor a reflection, but something based on external statements. I never found a compromise between their right and their wrong. After being expelled from religious institutions more than once, I went to a state school where, to my surprise, I could choose between different types of religious practice. I wish I had attended all of them and been able to understand the roots of various belief systems.

Since ancient times, besides various religions, philosophers have also written about happiness. Plato, Aristotle, Socrates and others have shaped centuries of reflections, and their works are still studied today. Philosophy was my favourite subject at university, not only because I had a passionate professor, which always helps, but because I had a fascination with the question of existence. I was searching for guidance in readings by Hegel, Kierkegaard, Kant, Descartes, Nietzsche and Marx. I was curious about everything, but my breakthrough came in 1991 when I decided to set sail, leaving everything behind, and embarked on a world tour to search for myself. This was not a stereotypical gap year; my studies were well behind me, and I had already been through six years of earning my living. But I was feeling a profound need to reset my clock. Beyond the great adventure, the encounters, adrenaline rush and new cultures, it was what I would describe as a spiritual journey. I was, and still am, a hedonist, an epicurean, a *bon vivant* inhabited by *joie de vivre*, a promoter of the *carpe diem* motto. But the quest for the purpose of human existence was a void in my life. The dimension of free thinking had been missing in my patchwork of experiences. I wanted to investigate this, starting from a blank sheet of paper, away from everything.

It was the most exhilarating and fulfilling journey. From the streets of Kathmandu to the beaches of Sri Lanka, from the trails of the Annapurnas to the emerald waters of the Siam Gulf, I reflected on metaphysical order and harmony. I immersed myself in the spirituality of Confucianism, Hinduism and Buddhism. I meditated through every sunset and read *The Art of Happiness* by the Dalai Lama. During the long train journeys across Indonesia and Malaysia, I read about Islam and enjoyed extracts from the Qur'an. The sound of peaceful prayers and my conversations with the locals made me feel like time was standing still, kind and never ending. People were not preoccupied by anything. When I sailed across Fiji, the Cook Islands and French Polynesia, I attended Mass in beautiful, simple beach chapels where every Sunday families gathered, dressed immaculately in white, with smiles of true happiness. It felt poles apart to me from the church where I had my confirmation. When I reached the end of my trip, coming up from Guatemala, Honduras and Cuba, I stopped in New York where the US Open was taking place. It was strange to be back in 'reality'. As I pushed the IMG office door open on 22 East 71st Street, a charming woman welcomed me, offered me a drink and invited me to take a seat. I had grown my hair, which had been discoloured by six months of rough outdoor living. I thought the company was delighted by the return of its prodigal son, but she had mistaken me for a pro tennis player coming to see his agent.

Yes, I was back in the 'real' world, but I had discovered new ingredients that had been missing in me: inner peace and wisdom.

Every moment is the destination

The world is not static. The search for meanings, answers and harmony never ends. Every year, I retire to a remote mountain lodge where there is no running water but a spring, no heating system but a log fire and only a couple of hours a day of electricity through a single solar panel that functions when it does not snow. You could not find a more different environment from the lifestyle I enjoyed for so many years. I have my books there, my music, a view of Mont Blanc. It is simple but spectacular. Today, I appreciate time without pressure – the most valuable commodity in life. It was in this environment that I wrote these reflections. I have been living in the fast lane as long as I can remember, but the time I cherish in my refuge is true luxury. I was on a constant quest for adrenaline, entertainment and professional achievement. I was driven, with no time to think about what it takes to simply feel good.

While in my hut, I read *Sapiens: A Brief History of Humankind,* by Yuval Noah Harari. The original pattern was basic: our instincts push us towards shelter, food, companionship and security. But as we advance in our civilizations, we become much more sophisticated. Nine billion years in the making for our little planet to coalesce. Another four billion years for life to inhabit it. And so many years for mankind to appear. But here we are: you, me, us, 'our' life, with its challenges and expectations, with its beginning and its end. Before we have the time to realize we are on a mission, the inexorable countdown has begun. Is this the harsh reality of existence?

Leonardo da Vinci wrestled with the concept of the moment. He compared an arrested instant of motion to the concept of a single geometric point. The point has no length or width. Yet if it moves it creates a line. 'The point has no dimension; the line is the transit of a point.' Using his method of theorizing by analogy, da Vinci wrote, 'The instant does not have time, and time is made from movement of the instant.' Inspired by such reflections, taken from the biography *Leonardo da Vinci* by Walter Isaacson, I see my precious little life in the grand scheme of space and time as a succession of valuable instants, and not a destination. Instead of imagining some undefinable 'goal' at the end of my life's journey, I realize that each instant of my life is, in itself, a destination. Instead of lamenting the passing of time, I would rather focus on making the most of every instant. It is a miracle that we even exist in the first place, and every single day the evolution of our fragile physical form is a miracle we take for granted.

What happened to me in the evolution of my ambitions was that I no longer looked only at childhood dreams or career accomplishments.

I questioned the fundamentals of what was driving me forward in this rapidly developing world. I could not be static. There is a strong and profound spiritual call, which was always there, which has grown increasingly loud. What is my legacy? What is my spiritual existence? What is my duty as a human being on this earth?

The call of duty

Looking at the acceleration of scientific progress and the ability of human beings to anticipate problems and find solutions, I am quite relaxed (though not complacent) about our future. I would rather use my time to focus on what I am able to contribute and enjoy a meaningful life at the same time. But how can you feel good when your brain is fed with facts and figures night and day that suggest the world is getting worse, and at a faster rate than ever before? Is it not irresponsible to take the view that things will be okay in the end?

Let's take the time for a quick reality check – what actually is the state of the world? While it's undeniable that there are still many issues worthy of time, energy, money and attention, it's also important to look at how far we as a species have come.

All the statistics I quote in the following paragraphs are taken from the book *Factfulness: Ten Reasons We're Wrong About the World and Why Things Are Better Than You Think* by Hans Rosling. The book – which I can strongly recommend – is a reliable source of data providing a positive outlook on life, as a counterbalance to the oversaturation of devastating news that we all face on a daily basis. It is a lot easier to be hopeful about the future when you compare the present with the past.

For example, the average world life expectancy today is 72 years – 25 years more than when I was born. Here's another: 86% of adults can now read and write, compared with 46% in 1960. And another: the proportion of people who can access safe water has gone from 58% in 1980 to 88% in 2015. Now, 80% of one-year-old children have had at least one vaccination. Do you think that in the last 20 years the proportion of the world's population living in extreme poverty has doubled, stayed the same or halved? You could be forgiven for believing that extreme poverty has doubled – but the actual answer is that it has almost halved. This bears repeating: extreme poverty is disappearing faster than ever before. And the world has never been less violent. Some 65 million people died during World War II, and we are living through the longest period of peace between superpowers in human history. Deaths from natural disasters account for 0.1% of total deaths. Plane crashes are responsible for 0.001%. Murder for 0.7%. Nuclear leaks for 0%. Terrorism for 0.05%.

In 1750, there were one billion people on the planet; in 1930, there were two billion, in 1970 three billion and in 1990 six billion. By the middle of the twenty-first century, there will be nine billion of us inhabiting the earth. Is this an opportunity or a threat? Should we sound the alarm bells? Well, the reality is that the population curve will almost certainly flatten. UN experts forecast that by the end of the century there will be between

10 and 12 billion people on the planet as growth begins to halt. More and more people, especially in developing countries, are being educated to have fewer children. The doomsayers say there will be too many people on the planet, and a catastrophic end is in sight for future generations – but birth rates in industrial countries are no longer increasing, and in some cases they are actually decreasing.

We tend to remember the bad over the good, sensationalist reporting sticks in our minds, and the spin of activists and lobbyists – no matter how well-meaning – can skilfully play on our fears. The alarmist exaggerations and prophecies of doom create an illusion of deterioration that increases stress levels and demoralizes even enthusiastic people. But, importantly, the smoke of drama is not only polluting our wellbeing; it also suppresses our appetite for endeavour.

It is so much harder to take action when you are paralysed by fear! It is harder to make a positive contribution to society if you are convinced that everything is going to turn out for the worst.

Optimism fires enthusiasm, which drives positive action to make the world a better place.

Digital devices

This all taps into one of my greatest fears for young people: addiction to their mobile phones. It's a spanner in the works of a progressive, productive life.

The average person spends approximately 2.5 hours on social media per day, burning the most valuable commodity in life: time. We are becoming slaves to our screens, sacrificing valuable time and energy that could otherwise be used in many positive ways.

The hours we spend on these addictive devices do not only financially benefit the rich white guys that sit behind these billion-dollar companies; they are a detriment to our mental health. We get sucked in and forget that the majority of what we see on these platforms is superficial at best and often fake, a glamourized view of the world that has been Facetuned and filtered.

Gen Z kids and their parents are having their brains hoovered by their mobile phones. There are benefits to this extraordinary world of technology and social media, but I fear there is also a detrimental impact on our mental health, wellbeing and privacy.

There is an opportunity cost to everything we do in life. Every second we spend on our digital device is time we sacrifice not doing something else. The engineers behind these revolutionary social media applications have designed a drug that we constantly crave, fostering digital dependency and creating a compulsive need to click and scroll.

From a chemical component perspective, there is an internal struggle between the four primary chemical triggers in our bodies: endorphins, dopamine, serotonin and oxytocin. Dopamine kicks in with a feel-good reaction when we complete a project, finish a task or reach a goal. It is the fuel to get things done.

We are social animals. We want to feel valued, and we want medals, titles, bonuses. We like awards ceremonies, graduations, memorials. We want 'likes' on social media, views on digital content and to feel a sense of reward through boosting the number of our 'followers'.

But the dopamine drip feed of digital dependency is making us unhappy, anxious, socially inept. How can we ever progress if we are constantly comparing ourselves with others and measuring ourselves against unrealistic standards of perfection? We are destined to develop an inferiority complex, anxiety and depression if we become distracted by validation through likes. You are not defined by how many followers you have or how many thumbs up you receive on a photo. The real world will judge you on your true character and emotional intelligence. Uniqueness and individuality are key ingredients to success. So why try to be somebody else?

The internet, online communication and social media have changed our lives in many positive ways. But taken to excess – almost to the level of an addiction – social media can be a distraction from real issues, the main one being the search for our true, unique personality. We need to discipline ourselves to unplug and realize that the truth lies within our environment, nature and our surroundings. We were here long before the internet and social media, and I sincerely hope that we will be able to find the power to distance ourselves from this artificial world which is impeding our personal growth.

These tech monsters are causing a loss of social skills, a loss of control and a loss of identity. It was already hard enough to find ourselves and develop as people. We now have an artificially intelligent force, so much more powerful than we are, playing with our natural instincts.

To young people, I want to say this: see the world through its true and powerful nature, not via distorted lenses. Be a version of yourself not influenced by robots. Listen to music, make love, go to bars, explore and live in the moment.

The world you came into was the fruit of the hard work and creativity of those who came before you. The lifestyle you enjoy is the gift of the previous generation. You have a duty not to break the chain. Respect the past to build the future. Don't lose yourself in scrolling endlessly.

Go back to basics: feel good about yourself, count your blessings, appreciate your environment, connect with others, enjoy the moment, while shielding yourself from the doomsayers. You need positive energy and a lot of it! The challenge of living a passionate and meaningful life will be impeded if you are consumed by depressing news and lost in a hall of infinite digital mirrors.

Before you give in to depression and gloom, look at the enormous progress that has been made and use this as motivation for the tasks ahead. It is a question of stimulating your purpose in life, embarking both emotionally and spiritually on the bandwagon of progress. You are born with a duty to contribute and you must use your energy and imagination to improve, starting with what you can do on your doorstep. This process of contributing and helping others might bring you contentment, as it did for me.

Do not underestimate the creative genius of humankind. Engage by contributing and making a difference. It can be something small or something big, on your doorstep or the world stage. But doing nothing is not an option. The search for meaning must lead us to hear the call of duty so we can leave a positive legacy. The good news – and I have experienced this – is that from a selfish perspective, the more you do the happier you will become.

Happiness is not a destination – it's an act.

CHAPTER 9

THE BUSINESS OF LOVE

Trying to find that elusive balance between work and life, professional success and personal contentment is one of life's great challenges, and many books have been written about it. Whenever I am asked to provide a short summary of my ideas on this, I fall back on a notion I have developed over the years about the 'three loves', which together make up the business of love. These are: love what you do; love the moment; love people.

Imagine a commodity that gives spectacular returns, outperforming any stock with no trading commission or financial risks. Imagine a pandemic that *encourages* social gatherings: the more you produce of this 'virus', the more contagious it becomes, and the more it makes the world a better place. Imagine a product that is organic, sustainable, with no polluting effect and in endless supply.

Imagine a commodity that costs nothing to extract, store or export, that is homemade, and where the more you supply the more you get back. There are no loan costs, no mortgage and no repayments.

In the world bank of love, the board of directors never cash in their bonus. It will keep paying dividends way after you have gone. To become a shareholder, you just have to join. Is there a downside to this idealistic notion of giving with no expected return? Is it a gamble? My journey of contentment was fuelled by the desire to give and share anything and everything: time, advice, opinions, feelings and support. I genuinely take pleasure in being generous and, without any expectations on my part, the returns have been abundant. I invite everyone to subscribe to this philosophy.

I have placed wrong bets, trusted the wrong people, been taken advantage of, burgled, attacked or beaten up, and my generosity has been abused. Yet it has never deterred me from seeing the good in people and their potential to reciprocate love and kindness. Simply put, love is the easy route to contentment.

This brings us back to the three loves.

Love what you do

Passion gives you wings. I cannot imagine going through the day without wanting to achieve something, and not simultaneously loving what it is that I am doing. There is a well-known saying: find a job you love and you will never work a day in your life. If you wake up in the morning with heavy feet, you may as well stay in bed. I genuinely find it sad to see people going through life without a passion, a purpose or an inner compass.

At the beginning of each year, I write a series of New Year's resolutions, and I continually update my beloved bucket list in an old notebook that has accompanied me for as long as I have had my old briefcase. It ranges from what books to read and films to watch, to the new passions to explore, the treks I want to try by bicycle, motorbike or on foot, planned reunions with friends, special celebrations to organize, new challenges – both physical and intellectual – and new businesses to start. I keep these lists updated, crossing off some items and adding new ones.

It is a real joy to put into practice. And it helps with adjusting to changing circumstances. It's also a way of making personal breakthroughs.

Love the moment

Live now. Don't regret yesterday, and don't wait for tomorrow; you don't know what is around the corner. *Carpe diem*. Remember: there is no dress rehearsal. Life is not all about long views or ambitious goals; it's about smelling the roses, the small experiences, the brief encounters, the good laughs, the good parties, the unexpected opportunities. Savouring the many moments in everyday life is an art. We waste too much time complaining, venting frustrations and envying others, but valuing simple emotions is a crucial part of life: walking in nature, cycling, listening to music, attending an exhibition, having a drink at the pub, going to the football, watching films and documentaries. It keeps your mind on a positive path of loving the moment and maintaining your happiness.

Love people

Connecting with people and developing a community of like-minded individuals who share your values, and with whom you have mutual love and respect, will boost your quality of life. Think about how much time you have on your hands, how it is spent, who you are with, the type and quality of relationships you have. Surround yourself with those you can lean on, share joy with and challenge yourself with. This is fundamental: we are not lone wolves. My only frustration when I did my solo world tour was that I did not have a companion to share my emotions with. I realized that I need to share the love of existence to be content, to feel part of a human chain.

This simple formula has provided me with guidance. It is my compass, an emotional bearing. It keeps my feet on the ground and my heart and mind in the right place. The three loves are simple investments, perhaps, but they provide great returns – whether in your personal or professional life.

CHAPTER 10

THIN LINE BETWEEN LIGHT AND DARK

I've discovered the key to happiness in life is simply this: think about what you have rather than what you don't have. Every day, be grateful for your ability to breathe fresh air, walk freely, feel, touch, kiss. Be grateful for being alive.

Mortality

I have experienced many things that have made me realize I cannot take life for granted. You may not recall your first friend, but the memory of Paul still lives with me. He was the boy I spent most of my time with from the age of eight; we decorated our bikes together, built dams, fished in local ponds with self-made rods, caught butterflies, had our first cigarette together. There was a bond between us. When he was about 16, he was diagnosed with a brain tumour. My first friend was violently taken away, after months of suffering. Baba was another friend, my mischievous partner in crime. He fell to his death during a climbing expedition on Mont Blanc at the age of 20. Jean-Jacques, my roommate at university in Namur, took his car one day and never came home. Xavier was one of us – six very close friends in apartment 216 at number 25 Grand Rue in Louvain-la-Neuve. We shared the same flat for three years at uni. His sister was my girlfriend. We were extremely close for 10 years, until he was taken away by liver cancer.

These losses hit me like one bullet after another. It became increasingly difficult for me to reconcile the paradox of the divine harmony of heaven and earth with the cruel injustices unfolding before me. More bullets whistled past my ears, reminding me of the fine line between life and death, happiness and sorrow. On the rainy afternoon of my 22nd birthday, from a telephone box I learned my mum had just had an operation to remove her breast. I hadn't known there was a problem. She was 43 at the time. Later, it was my turn to break the news to my own kids that their mummy was going to have chemo and radiotherapy, because we wanted to take the maximum precautions after the removal of a tumour in her breast. We were living a normal life without realizing we were actually in paradise, taking happiness for granted until we were forced to visit the gates of hell. I was very fortunate that both my mother and wife survived and got stronger through their experiences. Even during the writing process for this book, Kevin Roberts, who provided valuable editorial assistance to a man writing in his second language, passed away at the too-young age of 62. The bullets keep flying – I try to let them remind me to be grateful for the life I have.

Learning from my children

Alice is the second of our three children. To say she is engaged is an understatement. She is on a campaign trail on all fronts: human rights, anti-racism, equality for women, healthy eating. As she has grown into adulthood, she not only has my love but she has also earned my respect, because she is a woman of action. As head girl at school, she instituted a meat-free day, and lobbied to engage the school in sustainability programmes. She is involved in charities. She is currently writing a book about vegetarian cooking from her garden. I really love people who have strong opinions, but Alice is also a transformer and wants to make the world a better place.

One of my greatest pleasures and privileges in life is to walk with my three very different kids and enjoy philosophical discussions with them. Many of our conversations evolve around philosophy and living for a purpose. When I hear myself talking to them, I reflect on my journey, my education, the difficult experiences I went through, the challenges I overcame and the sacrifices I made. Often these reflections focus on the value of time, balancing hard work with fulfilment, the definition of happiness and what brings true contentment. To their questions of what I believe in, I say that ultimately I wanted to write my own rules, independently of outside influences, and to rely on myself. I wanted to direct my own life, draw my own map and write my own lines to find contentment.

My walks and talks with my children are a gentle way to learn about myself, but not all the lessons from my children's lives have been so gentle. One July morning in 2006, we were on holiday on the Belgian coast, and a violent storm was brewing. The blackness of the sky was merging with the greenness of the sea, and I called the kids to come and see – but when my four-year-old Louis ran towards me, he slipped, went crashing through a glass door, and impaled himself on a shard. The rest was a vision of agony. The sheet of glass cut deep into his throat, splitting his tongue and severing a branch of the carotid artery. I held him in my arms for 20 very long minutes, pressing into the wound to try and slow the bleeding as his face became increasingly white and lifeless. I will never forget the look in his eyes saying goodbye to me.

He had passed out when the ambulance arrived. Dr Hooghe operated on him in the ambulance before taking him to hospital. This little boy had lost 2.5 litres of blood; after surgery, he fell into a coma and remained on life support for a week. The whole time I was numb, in a different world. In January 2020, the same Louis, now a competitive ski racer and a true force of nature, was the youngest athlete selected for the World Junior Championships.

When driving together to and from his races, we reflect on the thin margin between missing a gate while skiing and winning the event, between success and failure, about what you learn from crashing into the snow – often more than what you learn from victory.

To me, his proud father, that sight in July 2006 epitomized the fragility of happiness. I still dream often about those events and how thin the divide between light and darkness is: from his early brush with death, Louis now lives his life as a bonus. He is a winner before he even starts because of what he has overcome, and everything he touches seems to be inspired by a supranatural power. As I write, he has turned 18 and is the last of my three children to leave childhood and become an adult, and still I am overwhelmed by emotion as I relive those dramatic minutes.

I am filled with nostalgia watching a video Alice compiled for her brother's 18th birthday. Looking in the rear-view mirror of life, I see waves of beautiful moments which made up our family life. I reflect on the concept of euhemerism and on the speed of light. And I think of how precious time is – don't waste it!

CHAPTER 11

NO DRESS REHEARSAL

So here we are, at the final chapter of the book. My hope is that you can take some inspiration from my journey, from the stories and thoughts herein, towards building, pursuing and living your own fulfilling life.

Take to the stage

Maybe I was born under a lucky star, I don't know; I have certainly had an interesting ride, and many incredible and invaluable experiences. I owe a lot to the people who gave me opportunities to thrive. I have been inspired by family members and influenced by mentors; I worked in the fray of industry pioneers. But I know that if I had not grasped these opportunities, and applied myself with curiosity, enthusiasm, an appetite for risk and a thirst for learning, it would not have mattered how many golden chances I was given – my life would not have been nearly as wonderful. When

I found my passions, I was determined to pursue my dreams. Being a possibilist and a positive thinker helped me to build my confidence and develop a unique profile, and I have used my emotional and social intelligence with relentless energy to gain a position in my community. I engaged wholeheartedly in the real world, and in a life of experimentation, progress and innovation that ultimately led me to leadership. Even if the best in the world had handed me a script, written me a role, or offered to open the stage door, ultimately no one but me could have taken to the stage. And the same is true for you – no one can play the role you play. You have to be willing to take that first step into the limelight.

Everything has led me here

I have always looked forward instead of back, broadly speaking, but after a few decades of this incredibly fulfilling journey I have taken time to reflect and ask myself whether, if I had to start again, I would do anything differently. Maybe I could have learned more languages, for example, or to play music properly. Maybe I could have started earlier – there are many choices I could have made differently. But in the end, I know I would not want to change the script. There is no point having regrets: I am profoundly content, and every choice I made has led me to this point. Honestly, I have had such a ball that I would give anything material I possess to buy myself another round on the carousel of life!

We all have moments of joy: landing a good job, lifting a trophy, getting married, receiving applause on stage. You will have your terrible moments too: losing that job, going bust, having accidents, grieving. But happiness is not a destination, nor is it a number at the bottom of a balance sheet. It is a practice, an action – an act. Finding your passion and building on it with determination are not just the path to professional success. Taking such an approach helps you find the right balance in all aspects of your life: romance, culture, entertainment, sport, spirituality and family. There is more than one path, direction, skill or journey. A multitude of dreams and opportunities are out there to be chased. However, you will always only have one life – so don't let the choices paralyse you!

Break out of your protective cocoon, build your confidence and leave your comfort zone. Unleash the tiger in yourself. Kill your demons. Seize the day.

The good life

What makes a good life? Everyone will come up with their own formula; as for me, I simply wanted to live my dream. As Bob Marley said, 'Live the life you love; love the life you live.'

Every step of the way, I challenged 'the norm' and wanted to maximize my potential in the quest for success and the pursuit of happiness. I sincerely believe that one does not go without the other. Success is not the key to happiness: happiness is the key to success. Don't feel you have to sacrifice everything on the way to gaining wealth, power or fame – these things can be marvellous, powerful drugs, but we all know the deep truth that, beyond the threshold of having your basic needs met, your degree of contentment is not determined by a bank account or the number of followers on social media. Live your passion, love and be appreciated, contribute and achieve.

You can make miracles happen. These are the components of a good and happy life.

Remember, you are the captain of your life, and you will decide how to navigate it. We decide what makes a good journey every day, and today is an important one: it is the first day of the rest of your life. Don't waste it.

We only have one life. There is no dress rehearsal.